LESBIAN AND GAY FAMILIES

LESBIAN AND GAY FAMILIES

REDEFINING PARENTING IN AMERICA

BY JILL S. POLLACK

FRANKLIN WATTS
The Changing Family
New York / Chicago / London / Toronto / Sydney

*This book is dedicated to my life partner, Jackie,
and our family.*

Library of Congress Cataloging-in-Publication Data

Pollack, Jill S.
    Lesbian and gay families : redefining parenting in America /
Jill S. Pollack.
      p. cm. — (The changing family)
    Includes bibliographical references and index.
    ISBN 0-531-11207-1 (l.b. bdg.)—ISBN 0-531-15749-0 (pbk.)
    1. Gay parents — United States. 2. Children of gay parents
— United States. 3. Parenting — United States. I. Title. II. Series:
Changing Family (New York, N.Y.)
HQ76.3.U5P65   1995
306.85 — dc20   94-23934
                                              CIP

CONTENTS

ACKNOWLEDGMENTS

Special thanks go to Tim and the parents of the Gay and Lesbian Parents Coalition International, who were always ready to provide information and to share their network of families. To Wayne, Sal, Sarah, Jim, Joyce, John, Diane, Lynette, and Julie, I owe a debt of thanks for the enthusiasm and life lessons you shared. I would also like to thank the many other parents who took time out to speak with me but, because of space limitations, do not appear in this book.

These lesbian and gay parents are brave pioneers. Likewise, Franklin Watts and the editor of this book, E. Russell Primm III, are to be applauded for their support and groundbreaking efforts to assure that a discussion of America's changing families includes those headed by lesbians and gay men.

Jill Pollack
Chicago
1995

CHALLENGING
TRADITION

After having been in a loving relationship for more than fifteen years, Wayne and Sal decided they wanted to adopt a child. They began researching the laws of adoption and the adoption process. They dealt with lawyers, judges, and social workers and two years later became the first openly gay couple to adopt in the state of New York. Their daughter, Hope, who is part African-American and part Hispanic, is now thriving in her new home with "Daddy Wayne and Daddy Sal." But researching and accomplishing an adoption hadn't been easy. Because there was such a dearth of information available to them, Wayne and Sal wanted to share all that they had learned of the adoption process and the special considerations of lesbian and gay couples. Their idea was transformed into an informational and social group called Center Kids, an organization in New York City for gay and lesbian parents and their children, which offers seminars on adopting and parenting as well as opportunities for these new families to share time together.

Joyce represents a far different case of lesbian and gay parenting. She did not conduct any research and did very little planning before she gave birth to her son, Michael, by alternative insemination, the process of impregnating a woman with donated sperm. Her lover at the time, Gail, was supportive of the whole process and its aftermath. But Joyce's parents struggled with both their daughter's lesbianism and with her wish to be an unconventional single parent. Following her instincts, Joyce created a different family structure. It includes her blood family and Gail, although she and Gail are no longer in a romantic relationship. They do, however, share a house. Joyce's son, Michael, knows that if Mom is not home, Gail will be there waiting for him. Michael's grandparents handle day care while Joyce is at work, and Michael even sees his biological father every week. An outsider might see so many people involved in raising Michael as confusing, but to him this is just a family.

While it's true that today's families are not what they used to be, these two families radically challenge the traditional notion of what it takes to bring up children. The structure and our ideas about what makes a family are being adjusted to reflect changes in American culture. While there are still many "nuclear" families consisting of one father, one mother, and children, there are nevertheless many other families headed by a single parent who may or may not be biologically related to the children. And there are also families with two moms or two dads. Medical technology has helped in this respect. Alternative insemination has created many options for having children without male/female intercourse. These options didn't exist ten or twenty years ago.

The parents I talked with for this book reminded me of how important family is in personal and political terms. Our families play an overwhelming role in the development of our values and our images of what sort of life we should lead. On a larger stage, parenthood is fodder for politicians and pundits alike. In fact, the very notion of "family values" has become a fundamentalist battle cry. But what exactly are family values? What is a family? And who should be allowed to have one?

Such questions are asked a lot these days. Not too long ago former Vice-President Dan Quayle blasted the television character Murphy Brown for having a baby and not being married. In several public speeches, Quayle connected having children out of wedlock with the breakdown of society. The argument has become a "hot button." Mention "family values" and you are bound to find strong opinions voiced on either side. Now First Lady Hillary Rodham Clinton is continuing the discussion about family values from a point of view far different from Quayle's. Her message is that a family is a family; that, "no matter what a family unit looks like today, the family remains the essential ingredient of shaping our later lives."[1]

The courts have joined politicians in grappling with the issue of defining a family. In 1993 several landmark cases had a profound effect on the families of lesbians and gay men. In Virginia, for example, a judge ruled a lesbian mother, Sharon Bottoms, unfit to care for her child, and based the ruling solely on Bottoms' sexual orientation. In fact, the judge gave custody of the child to its grandmother, who lives with a man who abused Sharon while she was growing up. The decision was later overturned, but Sharon Bottoms still faces months of appeals before her son can come home.

On the other hand, in Massachusetts, a judge ruled that both partners of a lesbian couple could jointly adopt their child. This has become an important legal precedent, for, in most states, two people of the same sex are not allowed to adopt the same child. Not only did the judge's ruling depart from this long-held view, but it also publicly acknowledged the couple's lesbian relationship to be a family.

Whatever the circumstances, a family is a family, no matter what its shape or size. This is especially important when talking about families headed by homosexuals, most of whom prefer to be known as lesbians or gay men. In 1979, *Webster's New Collegiate Dictionary* defined the term "homosexual" to

TERMS TO KNOW

Sexual Orientation —— referring to a person's self-identification as either homosexual, heterosexual, or bisexual.

Homosexual —— a man or woman who finds emotional and sexual fulfillment with members of the same sex.

Heterosexual —— a man or woman who finds emotional and sexual fulfillment with members of the opposite sex.

Bisexual —— a man or a woman who finds emotional and sexual fulfillment with members of either sex.

Gay —— slang term for a homosexual man or woman.

Lesbian —— a female homosexual. (The word is derived from the Greek island of Lesbos where a famous female poet, Sappho, wrote love poems to other women.)

Straight —— slang term for a heterosexual man or woman.

Fag (or Faggot) —— a derogatory term for a gay man.

Dyke —— a derogatory term for a lesbian.

Queer —— a derogatory term for a lesbian or gay man. (Recently this word has been reclaimed as a positive term by lesbians and gay men. It has even been used in the names of organizations such as Queer Nation, an activist group fighting AIDS.)

Come Out —— a slang expression for acknowledging one's homosexuality to oneself or to others.

mean exhibiting sexual desire toward a member of one's own sex. Today, the dictionary definition remains the same, but its connotations have changed. The word now connotes a person with the desire, or orientation, not only to have sex with, but also to live with and love those of the same sex. This enlarged concept of homosexuality, which is partly the result of decades of political action on the part of lesbians and gays themselves, encompasses a complete approach to life and love, not just sex. Although a full definition of homosexuality is still in flux and still a matter of debate even among lesbians and gays, for many it has come to represent a whole and complex identity.

The debate as to the cause of homosexuality has garnered much media attention over the past few years as scientific researchers have delved further into what makes the human body function. There are those who argue that there is a biological basis for determining sexual orientation, such as a specific gene. Others are convinced that individuals make a conscious choice as to whether they will be gay or straight (heterosexual). Still others believe that sexual orientation is determined by both biological and environmental factors. Some of us have a natural propensity to prefer intimacy with members of our own sex, yet environmental concerns, such as the current public code of morality or our upbringing, may play a large role in how we choose to express our feelings. It is very difficult to be sure of one's true sexual orientation when inner feelings conflict with social messages of right and wrong. Heterosexual unions still are considered the societal norm, and often any other type of union between two people of the same or opposite sex is considered a deviation.

Discovering one's sexual orientation can be a lifelong process. This is because sexuality exists on a continuum. Imagine a line with "homosexual" at one end and "heterosexual" at the other. While many people have feelings that fall close to one end or the other, many others have feelings that fall at points along the line. And the point at which we place ourselves on this line may change over the course of our lifetime. The feelings and attractions we have in adolescence may continue with us as adults. Or they may change as we become more familiar with the world and more comfortable with ourselves.

Expressing sexual feelings, especially if they are a little different from those of our peers, takes a lot of courage. Men and women throughout the ages have felt the need to cloak, or repress, their desire for members of the same sex. If they didn't, they were likely to face public humiliation, or even jail. In today's more tolerant climate, many have decided to "come out." The term "to come out" describes the act of acknowledging one's homosexuality to oneself or in a public manner. A person can come out to others on an individual basis or take a more public approach, such as sharing this information with the media, a school, a church group, or any other extended community. But each lesbian and gay man must decide for herself and himself when it feels safe and comfortable to share her or his sexual orientation.

The parents you will meet within these pages have all come out—some at very young ages and others much later in life. Some are "out" only to their family and intimate friends, others to entire communities. They come from all types of backgrounds, from small towns and from large cities across the country. In every case they have had to deal with the relationship of lesbian and gay identity to parenting.

Lynette and Julie are representative of one type of gay-parenting situation. They are raising their three adopted children, Keem, Quan, and David, in a small Michigan town in which they are one of the few African-American families. They both work in the field of child welfare and are well acquainted with how adoption courts treat lesbian couples. For this reason they chose to adopt their children in a different state, one with more favorable laws. They also decided not to disclose the intimacy of their relationship for fear that the adoption would be denied. Although Lynette and Julie are not "out" in their community, their relationship is understood by their children, who are now learning about how and when it is okay to share this information.

Diane also adopted her son, Tony, but under very different circumstances. Her life partner, Patty, who was Tony's biological mother, died two years ago from breast cancer. Now Diane is learning to be a single parent and coming face to face with the legal difficulties of justifying her relationship with Patty to the state government. Luckily, the support of both straight and gay friends and neighbors has given Diane strength in her struggle to keep and care for Tony.

Like Diane, Sarah didn't plan on becoming a single parent. But when the state threatened to put her sister's baby son in foster care because of signs of child abuse, Sarah accepted temporary custody of the child. Bryan is now ten years old, and Sarah is thankful to have permanent custody of her "son."

Many gay men and lesbians who came to terms with their sexuality later in life are raising children from previous, heterosexual marriages. For example, Jim knew he was gay when he was about ten or twelve but repressed his feelings long enough to have gotten married at the age of twenty-six. He maintains that he and his wife were relatively happy and had two children. But in his late thirties, Jim went through a period of depression, and from that point on, his marriage became more and more strained. After a few years of psychotherapy, Jim finally came out. He has separated from his wife but remains close to his children and active in their daily lives. Today, Jim and his wife are good friends, and he feels even closer to his children now that he is able to share his true identity with them.

John also married, even though he knew in his teen years that there was "something different" about him. Still, he wanted to have a home and a family and all the other things everybody else seemed to want. He and his wife started a family in the small town in which they had both been raised, but John knew there was something missing in his life. After accepting his homosexual feelings, he discussed the situation at length with his wife, and they negotiated their way through this foreign territory. It was two years before they told anyone that they would be splitting up. John waited until their two children were in high school and college before discussing his sexual orientation with them.

Each mom and dad interviewed tells a very personal story. Each has had her or his share of heartache, love, bad things, and good things. In some cases, the biological families of these parents chose to disassociate themselves because of "homophobia," or the fear of homosexuality. In other cases, open communication and unconditional love healed wounds and fostered a precious closeness among family members.

Although all of the parents were enthusiastic participants in the development of this book, a cloud of anxiety and apprehension hung over some of the interviews. Because of legal and social implications, only first names (and sometimes aliases) have been used to preserve confidentiality. The repercussions of speaking openly about being a gay or lesbian parent can be serious. Many states can remove a child from a gay or lesbian parent and, all too often, the sexual orientation of the adults involved affects child custody suits. Gay men and women who come out often face discrimination; they may be denied housing or get fired from their jobs.

The rich and honest narratives in this book are a contrast between these austere realities and the vivid joys and challenges of parenting. Whether these moms or dads are gay, lesbian, or straight, they all have favorite stories of their children to tell: tales of PTA meetings gone bad or those touching moments when they saw their child awake to the ways of the world.

As more women enter the workplace and America becomes more diversified, gender roles and assumptions about family are being reshaped. Many individuals are struggling to discover which new configuration will meet their needs. All this change can be frightening, yet change does not always signal something better or worse. It is just different. What makes a family work is the love and support each member contributes. Think about all the families you know. Regardless of their make-up, some are happy, some less so. But, however they define themselves, they are all families. Through these pages you will learn that families born of love are as strong as those created by blood.

It is my hope that you will read this book because you are interested in the changing families of America. Maybe you will read it because you are the child of a gay or lesbian parent or because you know someone gay or lesbian and want to learn more. In any case, congratulations, because your world will grow to include some very special people.

1
REDEFINING FAMILY

American culture is always changing, and new family forms are continually evolving. The reasons for this are many: increased career opportunities for women, improved alternative impregnation techniques, and economic feasibility all contribute to the changing American family. How many families do you know in which the father goes to work each day, the mother stays home, and everyone shares dinner each night? Granted, some families do still live by this traditional nuclear-family model, but many families now consist of friends, extended relatives, and significant others. Today's families include more than blood relatives; they are increasingly defined as intimate groups of people who love and support one another.

The redefinition of American families is a result of, in large part, society's willingness to consider the diversity of our population. There has been a lessening of intolerance against those who do not fit the "norm." For decades there have been households headed by single parents as well as lesbian mothers and gay fathers. But in the past, most of these parents—gay and lesbian included—had their children in heterosexual marriages. Today, gay and lesbian parents are more willing to come out, and in many cases they meet with broader acceptance.

For lesbians and gay men, the issues surrounding parenting are complex and sometimes disturbing. In addition to the emotional, financial, and legal considerations that face any parent, lesbians and gays must also face societal homophobia and the absence of equal rights in the eye of the law. Yet, the stories of Julie and Lynette, Wayne and Sal, Diane, Sarah, John, Jim, and Joyce are full of courageous acts and warm family events. Each has had very different experiences with legal battles. Each has found support in surprising places. Each has a different role with his or her biological family, and each has different concerns for the future. Together, this collection of stories tells a greater tale: that of gay and lesbian parents fighting as individuals for personal liberty and acceptance. It isn't how a family looks, it's how it works.

WHAT IS A FAMILY?

Over the course of this century, the definition of a family has widened little by little, despite resistance from religious leaders and a government that has been slow to recognize the change. There is no organized movement demanding alterations in how a family is defined. Rather, the move toward modified family structures is based on individual choice and circumstance. For example, women are now working outside the home in record numbers and building careers once open only to men. This affords them the economic strength and independence to have children on their own. Other notions once considered taboo, such as reliance on day care and housework by males, are becoming more and more popular as the number of single parents and two-income families rises. Medical advances, too, have expanded the definition of families and parenting. For example, alternative insemination now makes it possible for almost any healthy woman—single, married, or older—to become pregnant with donated sperm.

What impact do these changes have on American families? Plenty! Day care and equal opportunity for men and women are now part of the national agenda. Although "traditional" families abound, children with one parent or those born through alternative insemination are no longer "the only ones." Single-parent families are now documented by the U.S. Census Bureau, the agency responsible for conducting a census every ten years. And the numbers of unmarried women choosing to have children without plans for marriage continue to grow.

These examples are leading to changes in many people's definition of family. Yet in the United States, a host of laws and social expectations are still based on a traditional notion of family—that of a mother, a father, and children. It's true that fewer and fewer families fulfill this image, yet the legal system and social structures are resistant to change and remain committed to the old traditions.

Statistics show that of the nation's 91 million "families" in 1988, fewer than 27 percent fit the traditional nuclear family model.[1] Other families consist of same-sex couples, unmarried opposite-sex couples, single-parent households, or extended family households with grandparents, aunts, or uncles raising children. Many of these statistics are taken from the Census Bureau, which defines family as a group of two or more persons related by birth, marriage, or adoption, and residing together in a household.[2] A problem with this narrow definition, as with many statistics detailing family life in America, is that there is no allowance for lesbian and gay families. In a survey conducted by *Newsweek* a few years ago, however, a majority of people chose a very broad definition of family that read "a group of people who love and care for each other."[3]

Given that the government has created a definition for family that excludes same-sex couples, how do we determine the number of gay and lesbian parents in America? It is difficult to say exactly how many gay and lesbian parents there are. Although statistics collected by the government and private organizations can easily be found about almost any other family situation, the number of gay and lesbian parents can only be broadly estimated. First, the census and many other surveys simply do not give the option of listing one's household as a gay/lesbian family. Second, gay men and lesbians are often hesitant to come out to census and survey takers because they fear homophobia and discrimination. This is especially true when it comes to their rights as parents. Child custody and visitation rights are often in peril when one is identified as a lesbian mother or a gay father.

ESTIMATING THE NUMBER OF LESBIAN AND GAY PARENTS

As difficult as the number of lesbian and gay parents is to pin down, several solidly researched estimates have been attempted. The first was part of a famous 1948 study on sexuality that was conducted by the research team of Kinsey, Pomeroy, and Martin. Among their findings, they estimated that about 10 percent of the population had had a homosexual experience at some point in their lives.[4] Kinsey later reported findings from another study conducted from 1938 to 1963, in which nearly six thousand women were surveyed about their sexuality. This study concluded that 2 to 3 percent were exclusively lesbian and that 13 percent more had had lesbian sexual experiences.[5]

For many years, the idea that 10 percent of the population was gay or lesbian was promoted by some commentators. Today, many feel the actual number is probably less than 10 percent and is also in flux as men and women reevaluate their sexuality throughout their lives. If sexual orientation is a continuum, then many find themselves identifying at different points on the scale as homosexual, heterosexual, or bisexual at different stages in their lives.

Individual researchers, such as University of Virginia psychologist Charlotte Patterson, F. W. Bozett, Del Martin, and Phyllis Lyon, began to investigate gay and lesbian parents and their children in the hopes of finding solid statistics about this particular family arrangement and its sociological effects. Organizations also became interested. The American Bar Association, the National Center for Lesbian Rights, and marketing research groups such as Overlooked Opinions have issued their own findings on the number of lesbian and gay parents.

To date, the results have been rather disappointing. Because so many parents are unwilling to disclose their sexual orientation, the statistics gathered are, at best, estimates and the numbers from different studies vary. For example, researchers have estimated that there are about 1 to 3 million gay fathers and about 1 to 5 million lesbian mothers. If each of these parents has, on average, two children, the number of children of gay or lesbian parents is about 6 million to 14 million.[6] Yet another study, conducted in 1988 by the American Bar Association, concluded that there are 8 to 10 million children being reared in 3 million gay and lesbian households. This report also estimated that about 6 percent of the U.S. population live in gay or lesbian families.[7]

An interesting figure regarding lesbian and gay households was extrapolated from the 1990 U.S. Census. For the first time, respondents were given the opportunity to answer questions about nonmarital couple relationships. (These did not qualify as family.) In data collected from the twenty largest cities in the country, approximately 9 percent of unmarried couples acknowledged their relationship as same-sex couples. This data can be applied only in a limited sense and not to the entire population. The census did not count all gays and lesbians, only those who identified themselves as being in a same-sex relationship.[8] It also did not cover nonurban populations of gays and lesbians.

Determining the number of gay or lesbian couples that have children has also been a challenge. A 1990 survey conducted by the journal *Partners* concluded that 21 percent of lesbian couples and 9 percent of gay couples have children.[9] But even as we look at the limited statistics that are available, it is important to remember that it's not the number of lesbian and gay parents that is important. It is their right to equality and their right to raise their children without fear of recrimination.

Same Responsibilities, Different Rights

In the gay and lesbian community, men and women are realizing that the old rules do not apply anymore and that their parenting urges can be met. Internalized homophobia, which is the fear of identifying as homosexual because of one's own fear of homosexuality, seems to be on the wane among gays and lesbians. Community support networks have begun teaching that different does not mean wrong. These networks have expanded to include organizations for lesbian mothers, for gay fathers, for the children of gay or lesbian parents, and for lesbians and gay men interested in becoming parents. There are also organizations that provide outreach and education to schools, PTAs, and the public about lesbian and gay parents in an attempt to reduce ignorance and foster a better understanding of diversity.

Raising children in gay and lesbian families is becoming a focus for many gay and lesbian rights groups. Even such politically charged issues as gays in the military are beginning to receive less play than discussions of gay and lesbian families. Weekly newsmagazines are fond of printing polling results of public opinion about gays and lesbians having children or adopting. While these reports may be interesting, the fact remains that lesbians and gay men are forming families at a growing pace, regardless of the obstacles thrown in their paths. Having children outside of legally sanctioned marriage has never been easier or more popular. A decade ago, Wayne and Sal would have had little luck as an openly gay couple in their attempt to adopt their daughter Hope. Joyce decided that she wanted to have a child by alternative insemination. Her choice to impregnate herself without the services of a doctor would have been almost out of the question. But today, these phenomena, as well as the idea that Keem, Quan, and David have two mothers or that Bryan and Tony are being brought up by single lesbian mothers, aren't very unusual.

In examining the question of lesbian and gay parents, one might even question why it is important to talk about them as an identifiable group. They share the same joys and sorrows as most other parents. They watch their children grow and learn, go to school, have their first boyfriend or girlfriend, and maybe go away to college. But lesbian mothers and gay fathers face daily legal and social hurdles that heterosexual parents do not.

Today, the legal rights of gay and lesbian parents are being both reinforced and challenged. In any social movement, the temptation to focus on the setbacks and controversial cases often overshadows the immense progress and small steps to success and equality. In the past few years, antidiscrimination laws protecting gays and lesbians were adopted by many cities and businesses across the country. Domestic partnership ordinances are also on the books in about fifteen cities. Domestic partnership is a legal term awarding certain rights traditionally reserved for married people to unmarried couples, including same-sex couples. These rights may include medical insurance coverage, pension and retirement benefits, leave from work to care for a spouse or a member of the spouse's family, or various tax benefits. Recognition under the law as a couple carries a great deal of gravity. For instance, if one partner is ill and not fully cognizant, then under the law, a spouse may make legal and medical choices. Without recognition of spousal status, lesbians and gay men are faced with having to explain and defend their relationships at the moment that important, life-altering decisions have to be made.

Spousal or domestic partnership status can also convey certain benefits to the children of either partner. In most cases, this is still a few years away for lesbian and gay families. Each city has a different version of what domestic partnership means. Most versions are very limited in scope and pertain to benefits for city employees only. What is more, most states still prohibit two people of the same sex from adopting the same child, and a few states, such as Florida, prohibit adoption by homosexuals. But the courts have looked favorably on individual cases. For example, Illinois has followed the lead of Massachusetts and given clearance for two lesbians to adopt each other's biological child.

For many years after the gay and lesbian rights movement began in 1969, issues surrounding having and keeping children were not given priority. Basic civil rights first had to be won, reasoned most leaders. Twenty-five years later, basic civil rights for lesbians and gay men are not yet fully assured, but great progress has been made. Many members of the current generation have discovered that their sexual orientation does not preclude them from building loving families that include life partners and children.

Charlotte Patterson, known as a leading researcher of gay and lesbian parents and their children, reviewed more than twenty different studies about the children of gay or lesbian parents. In addition, in 1990–1991 she conducted her own research on thirty-seven children of lesbian mothers in the San Francisco area. Patterson concluded that gay and lesbian parents face many hurdles in addition to those facing all parents. She found that there was a wealth of information geared toward heterosexual couples considering parenthood, but next to nothing for lesbians or gay men interested in the subject. In an article for the *Journal of Gay and Lesbian Social Services*, she wrote, "The situation of lesbian and gay couples considering parenthood in the United States is best understood against the backdrop of pervasive heterosexism and antigay prejudice."[10] The prejudice Patterson refers to is found in virtually every aspect of life. The law of the land depends largely on a governmental definition of the family, which, as mentioned, does not allow for gays and lesbians. Taxes, powers of attorney, the right to decide health issues, inheritance laws, and even family discounts focus on this narrow, traditional definition of family. Diane, the woman who adopted her partner Patty's son after Patty's death, encountered such prejudice when she found herself forced to defend her monetary contributions to her relationship with Patty. If the two women had been married, under state law, Diane would have inherited Patty's possessions with no need to justify her income or her relationship.

This type of legal and institutional prejudice, or heterosexism as Patterson calls it, can be found in virtually any situation. School forms ask for information about the mother and father with no allowance for two mommies or two daddies. They also are written in a way that does not allow for single-parent families.

The rise in the number of single mothers in America has had a great impact on our ideas about family and on our ideas about lesbian and gay parents. Women who choose to have a child without a husband are bravely squaring off with those who deny a family is complete without all of its traditional parts. For lesbian and gay parents the challenge is an even greater one. Joyce, for example, is by all accounts a single mother. But her lesbianism places her in yet another class. Like many other single mothers, instead of receiving begrudging acceptance from society, Joyce must also face the possibility of greater discrimination in housing, in the workplace, and in such public accommodations as restaurants and hotels.

Then there are those subtle acts of discrimination and homophobia that are more difficult to evaluate—neighbors who prefer to keep their distance, PTA parents who discuss you behind your back, school systems that inhibit your child's ability to share her home life in the classroom.

A less subtle discrimination exists in the courts, where decisions of child custody or adoption are sometimes decided based on the sexual orientation of the parents. Blatant discrimination also exists in such organizations as the Boy Scouts of America, which specified that homosexuals cannot participate as scoutmasters or leaders. Even such public school systems as that of New York City have clearly shown their opposition to lesbian and gay parenting. In the early 1990s, New York was embroiled in a public debate about whether a "Rainbow" curriculum, designed to teach about diversity in families and society, should include discussions of homosexuality. The issue was a divisive one, and its repercussions are still being felt. In the end, it was decided that gays and lesbians were not to be mentioned. In fact, the school chancellor who championed inclusion of gays and lesbians in the Rainbow curriculum was forced out of his job.

Offenses such as these receive a great deal of public attention and are reported in the major media. But many gays and lesbians endure slurs and discrimination in the workplace and in social situations that go unreported and, in most cases, are not against the law. But their sting is felt deeply, and they do pose some strong challenges that gay and lesbian parents must overcome if they are to build healthy, happy, and integrated lives for themselves and their children.

Even in the face of public intolerance, lesbians and gay men are choosing parenthood in growing numbers. Although many homosexual parents, such as John and Jim, have children that come from prior, heterosexual marriages, others are looking to adoption, alternative insemination, and surrogacy as viable options. Both Patty and Joyce chose alternative insemination. Wayne and Sal and Julie and Lynette chose adoption. Patterson writes that an estimate made circa 1990-1991 held that five thousand to ten thousand lesbians have borne children after coming out in addition to the hundreds of gay men and lesbians who have adopted children.[11] Today, as alternative insemination techniques and access to adoption improve, that number is probably much higher.

THE CHILDREN OF LESBIAN AND GAY PARENTS

Not everyone believes that it is okay to be gay or lesbian or to raise children in a gay or lesbian household. For years, the American Psychiatric Association (APA) held the view that homosexuality was a mental illness. Although the APA revised its code book and no longer considers homosexuality an illness, many people still hold to the idea that it is a psychiatric disorder.

In response to a question about gay and lesbian parents, Joseph Knapp of the Family Research Institiute was quoted in *The New York Times* as saying, "We don't condone homosexuality in any way. We believe that being raised by homosexuals is detrimental to children. Our family values are a mom and a dad rearing the children."[12]

Historically, one argument used against gay and lesbian parents has been, "What will it do to the children?" For many years there were no scientific studies to back up either position of this debate. Emotionally charged religious and moral themes dominated the discussion. One side adamantly maintained that the Bible allowed for only a man and a woman lawfully and morally to raise children. Another side deferred to changing times and dismissed the idea of normal in favor of a closer look at the reality of the situation. It pointed out that people have been having children out of wedlock for centuries, that not all married parents are good, and that not all single parents are bad.

At the bottom of these disputes was the question of whether or not the sexual orientation of the parent would affect the child's sexual orientation or social development, as well as whether or not having homosexual parents would make life unduly difficult for the child.

For decades the courts reflected society's opinion that lesbian and gay parents were unfit without any scientific research to support their claims. Then, in the late 1980s and early 1990s, studies that compared children of heterosexual parents and homosexual parents began to appear. Their findings contradicted many of the myths about children of gay or lesbian parents. For example, unsubstantiated theories had always suggested that the children of gays and lesbians would have a more difficult time in developing relationships with other people, would grow up to be gay or lesbian themselves, or would be sexually abused or psychologically damaged. But according to the studies in the late 1980s and early 1990s, these assumptions could not be further from the truth. Study after study concluded that the children of gays and lesbians were no different from those of heterosexual parents. According to an article by Patterson in the journal *Child Development*, "Although studies have assessed over 300 offspring of gay or lesbian parents in 12 different samples, no evidence has been found for significant disturbances of any kind in the development of sexual identity. The same held true for moral development, intelligence, and peer relationships."[13]

Another study called "Homosexuality and Family Relations" was conducted by clinical psychologist Dr. Julie Gottman. She compared a group of thirty-five adult women with another group of thirty-five adult women who had been raised by lesbian mothers after a divorce from the father. Dr. Gottman found that on the whole, the group raised by lesbian mothers did not really differ from the other group in their "social adjustment or their identity as a boy or a girl." The children of lesbians were no more likely to be homosexual than those of heterosexual mothers.[14]

Together, these studies suggest that the children of gay and lesbian parents are just like any other children. They have normal relationships with other kids and adults of both sexes. They are also not at any greater risk for sexual abuse. (It has been proved that most sexual abuse is perpetrated by heterosexual men.) What is more, divorced lesbian mothers allow their children to see their fathers more often than divorced heterosexual mothers do.

Although scientific research strongly suggests the possibility of some genetic or biological basis for homosexuality, there seems to be no support for the idea that a gay gene is passed from parent to child. In fact, the studies mentioned above suggest that the sexual orientation of the parent does not have any bearing on the sexual orientation of the child. Just because your dad or mom is gay doesn't mean you are or will be. After all, the majority of lesbians and gay men have heterosexual parents!

Another group of researchers went one step further and wrote, "Children of gay men and lesbians are not different from children raised by heterosexuals but may adhere less to traditional sex-assigned societal standardism, and choose less traditional jobs. Five percent of these children reported harassment for their parents' identity. Parents' healthy self-concept is important for the child's healthy self-concept development."[15]

By saying that these children "may adhere less to traditional sex-assigned societal standardism," the researchers mean that these kids are less likely to grow up thinking that only men go to work each day and that only women stay home to cook and clean. As young children, they might also feel more comfortable playing with toys usually assigned to the other gender.

The new scientific studies have set the stage for you to learn more about Jim, Sarah, Diane, and the other women and men in this book—all of whom are parents in a society that sends confusing, mixed messages to them and their children. These parents have found their way with humor, with a healthy outlook, and with pride in their children and their accomplishments.

2
BECOMING PARENTS

If you asked most people how moms and dads get to be moms and dads, they might answer that a man and a woman have intercourse and, depending on several variables, the woman becomes pregnant. Nine months later a baby is born.

This scenario describes only one way to have a baby. Modern science and the legal system have created several options that are available not only to heterosexuals, but also to lesbians and gay men. Most of the parents in this book chose to have children and even picked the method that best suited them. Lynette and Julie and Sal and Wayne decided to adopt. Joyce decided she wanted a child through alternative insemination. Sarah and Diane hadn't planned to have a child, but both are thankful that one came into their lives.

Jim and John represent another category of gay parents: those who had children in prior heterosexual marriages. Sometimes this situation can cause much heartache, especially if the children are very young when the parents separate and husband and wife have different ideas about how they should be raised. But in other instances, the marriages are dissolved amiably. Sometimes relationships between parent and child are even strengthened by the open and honest discussion that occurs.

As we explore the options for becoming parents, you'll see that in many cases, emotions, the legal system, and biological family members are powerful players in deciding the fate of a child and her or his parents. You will also notice that all of these parents cherish their children and feel very fortunate about being a parent.

CHOOSING PARENTHOOD

As more and more same-sex couples and homosexual individuals decide to experience parenthood, it is becoming more obvious that their decisions are rooted in the same motives as those of straight men and women: the simple desire to raise a child and build a family. For many years, the gay and lesbian community felt that there was no place for children. This wasn't because lesbians and gay men doubted their parenting abilities. Rather, they assumed their lives would be so different from their heterosexual counterparts that children would not fit into the picture. Because marriage between same-sex partners seemed unattainable, a family also seemed out of the question. During those past times, marriage was considered the only "approved" method for having kids, so gays and lesbians learned to accept their "fate."

But attitudes change. When single women across America decided they could have children without having husbands, lesbians raising children from heterosexual marriages became more visible. Having children was becoming a viable option in the gay community.

The gay and lesbian civil rights movement contributed to these changes. With each battle, gay leaders widened their sights to include what had been considered unthinkable. In the fight against discrimination, for example, court cases developed around the plight of lesbian mothers fighting for custody of their children. This soon expanded to fighting for adoption rights as well. People began to realize that children were already a part of the gay community and that loving and nurturing were not characteristics of heterosexuals only.

Even after the choice to become parents has been made, gay men and lesbians face many important decisions. Because relatively few choose to have intercourse to produce a baby, other methods, such as adoption, alternative insemination, and surrogacy, are usually considered. Questions surrounding these choices include: Does the baby have to have my genes? Who would donate the necessary semen or act as a surrogate mother? How do I feel about adoption? Would I want a baby or an older child? What about the child's race or gender? Would I accept one that may have a disability or that carried "emotional baggage" from a difficult past? These and many other questions must be answered fully before anyone embarks on this adventure.

Adoptions

An increasingly popular choice for gay men and lesbians is adoption. Lynette and Julie chose to adopt their three children. As Julie tells it, Lynette was an administrator in a child welfare agency that frequently posted pictures of children who were waiting for adoption. Lynette saw the picture of Keem, Quan, and David on the wall. She came home screaming, "Julie, Julie, there's a great sibling group [brothers and sisters] on the wall, come and see them." She explains:

> [One day] I got up from my desk at work and trudged out in the cold to look at the three people on the wall. We looked at their records, and talked about them and talked about them. Both of us have been in the field of child welfare for ten plus years, and Lynn has a heart bigger than the state of Michigan . . . so we adopted them.

Adoption is the legal act of taking another's child as your own. This child then becomes your responsibility and your legal concern. The questions facing a prospective adoptive parent are crucial; their answers will affect not only the adult, but the child as well. For gay men and lesbians, the questions multiply, and the answers often smack of compromise. For example, in most states, two people of the same sex cannot become the legal parents of the same child. This means that same-sex couples must choose one partner to be the legal parent, leaving the other partner in an awkward legal position. Although some say this distinction is only on paper, a closer look reveals that this legality has some major consequences. What if the "legal" parent dies? The child could become a ward of the state and be taken away from the person that the child has known as the other parent. Prospective parents must also consider the legal climate of the state in which they live. Is it legal for an openly gay person to adopt? Is there any hope for a second-parent adoption so that both parents will have a legal standing with the child? Is there anyone who might contest this action?

Even though some states, including Florida and New Hampshire, prohibit adoption by gays or lesbians, individuals still proceed in doing what they feel is right. In cases such as Julie and Lynette, sexual orientation may have to be hidden. Couples must also resign themselves to having only one legal parent while retaining equal parenting responsibilities in the home.

Having to lie about being gay—or worse, being "found out"—is a major concern for all gay or lesbian parents. Fortunately, the national atmosphere is improving, as demonstrated by cases in Massachusetts and Illinois. In 1993, a Massachusetts judge recognized two lesbian partners as the legal parents of the young child they were raising together. This public recognition of their "family" can now be cited as a legal precedent in support of similar adoption cases. A year later in Illinois, a judge cleared the way for another lesbian couple to proceed with hearings to adopt the two children each had by alternative insemination. (The final adoption is still pending.) Additionally, an increasing number of state agencies and adoption programs are recognizing that gay and lesbian parents can provide nurturing and supportive homes for the many children who need them. Still, as with most social change, legal victories are tempered with setbacks. It is still true that lesbians and gay men are too often discriminated against in adoptive proceedings and, especially, in custody battles.

Recently, in Virginia a judge ruled that a lesbian, Sharon Bottoms, was an unfit mother for her two-year-old son based solely on her sexual orientation. The case was initiated by Sharon's mother, who asked for custody of the child. The judge's ruling was appealed and a higher court granted Sharon custody. Unfortunately, her mother appealed the ruling of the higher court and Sharon must wait until this legal battle is settled before her son can come home.

Whether they are gay or straight, would-be parents need to prove to the state that they are fit for the job. Some states require that prospective parents be certified as foster parents before they are allowed to adopt. This means answering extremely personal questions about one's life history and current lifestyle. It also means submitting to home visits by social workers who evaluate what kind of atmosphere the parents would provide for the child. Next, formal adoption proceedings must be initiated. The case will go before a judge who will rule whether or not the adoption becomes final. Lynette and Julie say they were fortunate to have had a judge who understood their situation from what was *not* said, rather than from what was said. She understood that Julie and Lynette would be partners in raising the children.

At several points in this process some gay or lesbian couples feel the need to lie to visiting social workers, or omit certain details. This is because coming out as homosexuals would immediately disqualify them as parents. The increasing number of placements in gay homes suggests that state-run adoption agencies are beginning to agree, at least tacitly, that sexual orientation does not affect parenting skills and that gay men and lesbians are very often a good match for a child. Private adoption agencies, however, are not bound by the law to consider lesbians and gay men for adoptions and are often more discriminating in choosing parents.

The legal entanglements of adoption can become very complex. Add to this the lack of legal standing afforded to gay and lesbian families, and a host of obstacles can present themselves. To guard against this, many couples are very cautious when preparing to adopt. Wayne and Sal, for example, decided that Wayne should be the legal parent because his job with the state of New York has excellent health insurance benefits that would extend to their child. If Wayne died, Hope, as his dependant, would still be entitled to the health insurance and any other well-being or monetary benefits Wayne's employer might provide to family survivors.

Wayne and Sal were this thoughtful during every step of Hope's adoption. In fact, after deciding that they did indeed want to adopt a child, they conducted thorough research on adoption. This preparedness gave them advance notice of what they could expect from adoption agencies and the courts.

Wayne's and Sal's parenting odyssey began with a period of acting as "alternative parents" for a teenager who had nowhere else to go. Wayne tells the story this way:

> We got a phone call saying there's this homeless kid, who was thrown out of his house because he was gay. He's too old to be in foster care, too young to be an emancipated minor. The only place that he could possibly go was one of the city shelters. Would we give him a place to stay for a couple of days, or a couple of weeks?

Joey was seventeen and a half when we met. We really hit it off, and we gave him a level of stability that he had never had. He had been in and out of foster care all of his life. His father was killed when he was very young and his mother was in and out of mental facilities. He had a real troubled upbringing.

They hooked us up with him because Sal and I both knew sign language, and Joey was profoundly hard of hearing. We had his hearing reevaluated. He got a new hearing aid and soon he was hearing 90 percent of normal [in one ear].

I guess we were role models for him. We showed him a gay community that he didn't know. He knew the streets and he knew the bars. He didn't know about the organizations that our community had set up.

Although this trio had some rough times, Wayne and Sal were able to provide Joey with a stable home life. They gave him the tools he needed to make his way in the world as an adult.

He finished his GED [a high-school equivalency certificate], picked a career, and started to pursue that. The only reason he moved out was because he met a lover who had an apartment and could help him. We were together about a year and a half. During this time, these parenting urges came out in me that I never knew I had. I came to further understand, yes, we can be parents and be rather successful at it.

After having this epiphany, Wayne attended a workshop for gay men considering parenthood. He says the workshop affirmed for him that there is a place for kids in the lesbian and gay community. After running into a lesbian couple who thrust their baby into his arms, Wayne says, his "fate was sealed. I came back to New York from the conference, and Sal picked me up at the station. I didn't say hello, I didn't say

38

how are you doin' ? I said 'Let's do it!' He knew exactly what I meant."

Once the decision was made, Sal and Wayne set about researching their options. They learned about public and private adoptions and tried to get information specifically geared to gay and lesbian parents. They found very little. Although they contacted a few gay adoptive parents, they had to concede that they were entering uncharted waters.

We went into this with a great deal of forethought. We realized that we were sort of untraditional. We didn't want to [mistakenly] do something that would prevent us from adopting. There were issues that had to be raised: Were we going to do it openly gay, or were we going to be covert in any way? I've always said, after fifteen years of being totally out in the open under every circumstance, how can we possibly not? What kind of message would you be giving your child if you're not going to tell the truth? If you could not be open about your being gay, then you're giving a mixed message to your child that it's okay to be gay in certain situations and not in others. And to me that was very contradictory; it just does not make sense.

We had to start talking about basics. We decided we didn't care about the child's gender. We didn't care about the child's race. We were not necessarily looking for a newborn, but we wanted a child who would join our family before starting school. That was the only real limitation. We were willing to take a child with a handicap so long as that handicap was not a total disability. We wanted a child who would grow independently.

We had one issue that was very difficult to resolve and that was one of religion. I'm Jewish; Sal's Catholic. It was by far the last issue that we had to resolve, and it took a long time to do that. I consented that it was all right to raise our child Catholic so long as all of a sudden we didn't "find religion." We don't go to church every Sunday. We go for Easter and Christmas. We celebrate whatever holidays are appropriate.

We realized that there's a number of different ways to adopt. The public system didn't cost you anything. In fact, they even paid you for a while. You can go independently or international and it costs huge sums of money. The city assigned us to this agency, and it turns out that the agency was affiliated with Catholic Charities and the Brooklyn Diocese. We thought we were shot down before we even started. But we're very lucky in having had an adoption supervisor who understood that New York State has an executive order that protects us on the basis of sexual orientation.

The regulations around adoption are very specific. Homosexuality cannot be the sole reason for denying the placement of foster care. Suffice it to say, they treated us as a gay couple. We had very liberal social workers who were very comfortable working with us, and both the adoption supervisor and our social worker understood the sensitive issues that we were going to deal with. They even shielded us from some of the discrimination that was existing in their own agency.

We had to go through a home study which is intense. [They] wanted to know our entire life history. They viewed us as a couple, so they first went through Sal's whole life, then my whole life, then they dealt with our life together. They asked questions on our backgrounds, how do we settle disputes, how discipline was dealt with in our homes, is there any alcoholism. The whole purpose is to find out your suitability as parents. I have to say that ours was a glowing home study. It was longer than most traditional home studies, but they felt they had a point to make. We came out like the Ozzie and Harriet of gaydom. That, at least, got us on our way, and we were certified as prospective adoptive parents.

New York requires that the child reside with you for six months before you can petition to adopt, so technically you're certified foster parents until you can do that. We now have the state granting the two of us together since they certify the household regardless of who's in it. Then we were free to look for kids. New York State has its lists of waiting children in what are called Blue Books (the covers of the books are blue). It's basically like the Sears catalog of waiting kids. There is a photo and a caption, and some sort of description of what the child is about. Then you play God.

Over a space of eight months, we identified twenty-four kids in the Blue Books that were of interest to us. Each and every time we received a similar response to our inquires that we were unsuitable for the child. Then we realized that there was a great deal of homophobia going on. We were just about ready to file a class action suit when we got a call from our agency saying would we be interested in a four-and-a-half month old little girl? We were not the first people they called. No one else seemed to want her. She was abandoned at birth by her biological family. The mother was using cocaine during pregnancy and she, my daughter, tested positive to cocaine upon birth. She also had some physical delays . . . it was called floppy muscle syndrome; the muscles were not developing equally.

At this point, Wayne and Sal discussed the possibilities. Both men had backgrounds in special education, and they knew where to turn for help and information. A few days later, the little girl was placed in their home. Wayne and Sal performed therapeutic exercises with Hope, and within six months, all of her physical problems corrected themselves. Wayne proudly says, "Our family began August 19, 1987, when she was placed with us."

Sarah also faced complex court proceedings before finally obtaining permanent custody of her son, Bryan. Unlike

TERMS TO KNOW

Alternative (or Artificial) Insemination —— using a medical procedure to inject semen into the uterus for the purpose of becoming pregnant.

Adoption —— the act of legally accepting a child as one's own; to be legally, financially, and emotionally responsible for one's non-biological child.

Foster Parenting —— providing a nurturing and stable home for an orphan or a child in need of a temporary home.

Surrogacy —— when one woman bears a child on behalf of another man or woman, sometimes from her own egg fertilized by the semen of a donor.

Sperm Donor —— a man who gives sperm for use in alternative insemination.

Sperm Bank —— a facility maintaining donated sperm for use in alternative insemination.

Wayne and Sal, however, Sarah had virtually no warning that she would become Bryan's mother. After a call from her sister, who was Bryan's biological mother and lived in another state, Sarah learned that Bryan, then only eighteen months old, was going to be taken away from his mother and placed in foster care. A few days later Sarah traveled halfway across the country.

I think it was September 23rd. I got a phone call from my sister that there was a family crisis. She reported that her son, Bryan, was in the hospital, and they were accusing her of child abuse. I was on a plane three days later, went to court, and came home with a kid. I had no idea whether I would have him for a week, a month, six months, or a year.

He was severely abused physically. He was taken away by the county because my sister and her husband were charged with neglect and abuse. First, he was in the hospital but then he was placed temporarily in foster care, and he would have remained in foster care during the duration of the case. I didn't know how long it was going to be, so my natural inclination was to say, I'll take him. I don't want my nephew in foster care. My sister never really came out and said, Sarah, will you take him? I think it was just her unspoken desire. She was in a crisis and she also did not want Bryan to be in foster care. Later she expressed that she was grateful that I took him. I don't think she believed, at that point in time, that the situation would have evolved how it has. She probably could never get him back even if she wanted to.

To take Bryan home with her, Sarah first had to get legal custody of him. This does not mean that she was adopting Bryan, just that she would be his temporary legal guardian until other arrangements could be made. The fact that Sarah lived in a different state than the baby made the court proceedings a little unusual.

The remarkable thing is that they broke the rules. Legally, a child is not allowed to be released outside of the county, even to a family member, without doing a home visit. Just because I'm blood, doesn't mean I'm a suitable parent. The judge felt strongly that this child had been through so much and that the foster care system is such a terrible place. Why should this kid be subjected to anything else.

I got temporary custody—now, I have permanent custody. Temporary custody meant that there was a still a case going on. It meant that I could make all the decisions, I was his bona fide legal guardian. But over the range of time defined as "temporary," custody could be taken away. It could be given back to the parents or to somebody else.

Permanent custody means that the case is closed. That my sister and her husband have surrendered—they had to. The court took away their custodial rights, but the state still recognizes them as the parents [although Bryan's father has since died]. Were the court to have made Bryan eligible for adoption, first it would have had to revoke my sister's and her husband's parental rights. We're talking about something that's not really tangible. Yet, it has a tremendous impact on Bryan. Permanent custody means that they could come at any time—either the dad or the mom—and say to the court that they think they've got their act together enough to be parents and petition the state for custody.

Getting to this point was an ordeal for Sarah. She had to traverse the legal system across state lines and face some unknown variables. Her lesbianism became an issue during the case, although it was not a major factor in the court's decision.

They put me through no kind of questioning. But I had to hire an attorney. I thought I had to hire an attorney for my sister. I don't know who's the perpetrator of the abuse but I know that she's in trouble. I know that her husband has just been released from prison, and I know that there are multiple boyfriends involved. I contacted two communities to get referrals for a lawyer, the Jewish community and the gay and lesbian community. The woman I chose was a lesbian. After I said I wanted her to take the case, she said, "Okay, now that you've decided this, I'm not going to go to court with you because I'm a woman and I look very masculine and you're going to court in a rural county. I'm going to send my legal partner with you who is a man."

44

At first I was a little put off by it but I thought, "We really want what's best for Bryan." I never said anything to him [the lawyer] about being a lesbian. I was Bryan's aunt and my sister's sister. Minutes before we went into the courtroom, the dad showed up—the dad who had been released from prison. My sister feared he was trying to find her. In fact, he tracked her down and showed up at the courthouse in a very dramatic way. Moments before we walked into the courtroom, he apparently told the county social worker that I was a lesbian and that there was no way on God's good earth that he wanted his son to go with me.

As we're sitting in the courtroom, my sister turns to me and tells me this. I'm sitting in a courtroom that is deciding the fate of my son—(I call him "my son" now)—and I hear the social worker objecting to my taking Bryan. I immediately assume that he's objecting because I'm a lesbian. I can't talk to my attorney because he's across the room, but I pass a note saying, I'm a lesbian and I think this might be why the social worker's objecting and we need to fight this.

It was never mentioned again. But, the threat that my lesbianism could be used against me to prevent me from being a parent came up right away. It haunts me. I immediately had to take a look at what my involvements were in the gay and lesbian community because I didn't ever want anybody to take Bryan away from me because I was a lesbian. I became really very careful about it. I didn't go back into the closet. I didn't really stop being involved, but I was careful.

Sarah became more careful about appearing in any print media and more cautious about coming out to people at work. But she continued her involvement in other activities she considered to be more private. For instance, she remained very active in the gay and lesbian synagogue.

In hindsight, Sarah counts herself lucky to have been

given Bryan as a part of her life. Her legal standing with him is sound for the present, and Bryan has even asked to change his last name to match hers. Yet the threat of future legal action lays in wait. It will probably not disappear from Sarah's worries until Bryan's eighteenth birthday.

Other lesbian and gay parenting opportunities that are sanctioned by the legal system include foster parenting and surrogacy. Foster parenting, as briefly mentioned above, is an excellent first step for those considering adoption. To become a foster parent, one must register with local authorities (usually the county or state) and sometimes submit to a short training and orientation program. Once approved and certified, foster parents may be called on to house a child or children, for a day, a week, or months at a time. A small stipend is paid to the parents to help with food and clothing costs.

It is not unusual for foster parents to become attached to a particular child and initiate adoption proceedings. The same rules that applied to Wayne and Sal, including home visits, would apply for these prospective parents. It should be noted, however, that, as with adoption, certain state laws apply. In some political jurisdictions, lesbian and gay parents are, by law or by legal precedent, not permitted to become foster parents. New Hampshire, for example, bans lesbians and gay men from becoming foster or adoptive parents. South Dakota requires foster parents to be married. This, of course, effectively bars homosexuals, who cannot get legally married.

But legal and political climates do change. In 1985, Massachusetts regulated that lesbians or gay men could not become foster parents. Eventually, the prohibition extended to adoptions as well.[1] Yet, as we discussed earlier, just eight years later a Massachusetts judge reversed this prohibition and allowed two lesbians to adopt a child.

Surrogacy

Surrogacy refers to an agreement (often a written contract) between two parties: a woman surrogate, who agrees to become pregnant and carry a baby to term, and an individual or couple who will become the adoptive parent(s). The surrogate agrees in advance to give up all rights to the child as soon as it is born. A medical procedure called alternative insemination is used to impregnate the surrogate. In the gay community, surrogacy has become a viable option for gay men and lesbians who wish to raise children. In these cases, the child is often conceived using the sperm of the gay father.

Unfortunately, there is still some controversy surrounding the issue of surrogacy. Celebrated cases have detailed the predicament of both parties when the surrogate, who had agreed to a contract, suddenly decided she did not want to give up the child. When it comes to human life, even a signed and sealed contract cannot always guarantee which parent will ultimately retain legal custody of a child. Still, many people are willing to take the risk.

Some gay men do have sex with women and some lesbians do have sex with men. Identifying as lesbian or gay does not mean that one's sexual partners are restricted to those of the same sex. In many instances, gay men and lesbians decide to conceive children through intercourse. In these cases, there are many options for raising the child. He or she may live with one or both biological parents. The child may even be raised by a combination of the biological parents and their life partners. In essence, the child is raised in a family, however these people define it.

Alternative Insemination

Alternative insemination (also called artificial insemination) is a miracle of modern science. The basic process involves putting semen into the vagina using a device similar to a syringe. Over the years, this process has become so simple that many women do it in the comfort of their own homes. Or they can choose to have a doctor or technician perform the procedure in a medical clinic. Many lesbians and lesbian couples are choosing this pregnancy method. A support network of mommy groups and advocacy/information organizations dealing with alternative insemination has popped up across the country.

The pros and cons of alternative insemination pose many questions. For example, the cost of the procedure is prohibitive for some women. In addition, because alternative insemination was historically done only by a physician, many doctors still feel they should have the right to decide who is fit to become a mother and will not inseminate lesbians or single women. These decisions are based on the personal beliefs of the individual doctor. In the United States, there are no laws barring lesbians from becoming pregnant by this method. But in France, the insemination of older women has caused an uproar and even led the country to pass a law denying this option to single women and to women over a certain age.

Other legal questions can arise regarding the rights and responsibilities of the man who donated the sperm. Many sperm banks pay accepted "donors" a small fee. These donors are screened for a family history of disease or illness, and they are also tested for AIDS. In many cases, donors do not have any contact with the potential mother before or after the insemination. Some sperm banks, however, are beginning to give the donor the option to be contacted later should the child, or the child's mother, wish to contact him.

For lesbian mothers, the decision of whether to use such a facility or perform the insemination themselves is often not an easy one. There are health centers that offer insemination services that are sensitive to lesbian concerns. But some still refuse to work with lesbians. These and other considerations led both Joyce and Diane's partner Patty to pursue pregnancy without the assistance of a formal clinic. Diane explains why Patty pursued this method:

> For a lot of lesbian families, the decision to have kids is a joint decision just like in heterosexual marriages. For us, it

didn't happen that way because I didn't meet Patty until she was six months pregnant. She had always loved children and had lived with friends who had kids. She was in a relationship with a woman who didn't want to have children, and when they broke up, she decided that if she was going to have kids, she was going to have to take the responsibility to do it herself. She really wanted kids and thought she'd be a really good mother. So she made a decision on her own and then went about it.

Patty wanted to use artificial insemination, not the old fashioned method because she wanted a kid not a father. I think it took her two to three years before she was finally successful in finding a way to do it. She said she was very frustrated until one day she connected with a friend of a friend who told her about a group of women in Seattle who did artificial insemination privately. She went out there . . . had two different inseminations, and she got pregnant. She didn't go out there on the optimum week [for getting pregnant]. She went the only week she could get off work. It was by accident that she was out there at the right time.

It can take several inseminations before a woman becomes pregnant. Patty was very lucky to have gotten pregnant so quickly. Joyce was also lucky enough to get pregnant after only one insemination. She was adamant about not wanting to submit to the rules or whims of a doctor. She had always wanted a child, and without much forethought she artificially inseminated herself with the donated sperm of a friend and coworker, and the help of her then lover, Gail.

Somebody told me that you have to take your temperature in the morning before you wake up to see when you're ovulating. So I kept a thermometer in a nightstand drawer, and I would reach for it every morning for eight months. One of my friends was having artificial insemination, and she was going to a doctor.

She gave me the [temperature] charts, and after a few months, she looked at my charts and said, "These are the goods days to do it."

I knew the father—we were friends and started working together. He had very dark hair and very dark eyes and I thought he was cute and nice. That was all. We were getting to know each other, and I said, "I want to have a child by the time I'm thirty. Would you like to donate some sperm to me? I don't really want anything from you . . . except if he wants to meet you, I'd like to introduce you to him." He said, "Fine."

Gail didn't like it. She didn't believe that he was just going to be a donor. She said, "He's going to see you every day. He's going to see you getting pregnant. You're going to get bonded to this child, and I don't believe that he's not going to have any effect or anything to do with this child." She wanted it to be me and her.

After we artificially inseminated I continued taking my temperature because, who thought in a million years it was going to work. But it did. I knew I was pregnant, probably within four days. I went to a doctor for a pregnancy test, and he couldn't believe it. People thought it was such a weird thing to do but, of course, it wasn't a weird thing to do. It makes perfect sense. Who needs the medical profession to do things like this.

Joyce's parents didn't support her desire to be a single mother, and throughout the pregnancy, there was much discord and discussion on the subject. Finally, Joyce was estranged from her parents until she went into premature labor.

It was a horrible pregnancy. I was sick every day. I was miserable. I was stressed. I was having anxiety attacks. I went into premature labor—I was [only] seven months pregnant. They stopped it, and I stayed in the hospital about a week on bed rest. Then I was on bed rest for two months at home. My parents did come to the hospital, and I started resuming some type of family relationship, especially with my brother and sisters. They didn't think I was doing the wrong thing. They were pretty liberal. I have two sisters who started visiting me when I was laying in bed. They were into it because it was the first baby [in the family]. It was interesting. It was fun having the first one. It was very exciting.

After weeks of bed rest, labor pains signaled that it was time for Michael to enter the world. Once he was born, Joyce's family came back together. Today, her parents are very involved in Michael's life.

Heterosexual Marriages

Joyce chose to have her baby in a very unconventional manner. Jim and John each chose to have children in conventional heterosexual marriages when they were in their early twenties. Both men lived quiet lives in nuclear families until they came out of the closet as gay men many years later. Like other lesbians and gay men, Jim and John had to deal with their own issues of coming out, and at the same time had to consider the effect it would have on their spouses and children. A divorce is not always imminent, although this is the solution for most couples in this situation—just as it was for Jim and John. A divorce raises many crucial issues. If the children are young or still of school age, is it better that they stay with the mother or the father? If the couple's relationship is not amiable, they might even find themselves in court fighting over custody.

But other couples are able to work through their differences. John and his wife dealt with the impact of his homosexuality on their family one step at a time. John feels that his road to fatherhood was the same as that of many of his high-school friends. Then suddenly he and his wife were playing without the usual rules or role models.

When I got married it was 1965, I was twenty-two and she was nineteen. We had two children. One was born a year after we were married, and the second, two-and-a-half years later. During that period of time, it seemed like everything was going the way it should. I had a job I loved, and I loved my kids and my wife. Economically things were working, and communitywise things were working and I felt very solid.

About three or four years after my daughter was born, marriage problems started happening. We both started wondering why certain things were missing and didn't know why. I thought, "Maybe I am different." The type of experiences I had as a younger person negated my thoughts about the fact that I might be homosexual. However, now as an adult, what I was finding in my investigation was that suddenly there was a more comfortable place for me.

Coming out was only the first step. Next John had to determine how to keep his family together but still lead a satisfying life. He continues:

The question was, "What do I do with all of this?" Since I was in a family situation where I had certainly loved my wife a lot and respected her and wanted the best for her, I didn't want to break everything up. We took about two years before we decided what it was that we were going to do.

John was very lucky in his relationship with his wife. Jim's story is similar. He credits his wife with accepting his homosexuality and working with him to provide the best possible environment for their children. Both men's wives came to terms with the fact that their husbands would not be happy remaining in the marriage. Although this took its emotional toll, each husband and wife discussed it openly. They were able to plan and strategize ways to meet their own needs while continuing to provide a nurturing and loving environment for their children. Today, both men say they have very open and positive relationships with their children and their ex-wives.

Twists of Fate

Tragedies come in all varieties and hit all types of families. Sometimes a parent becomes ill or a child is a victim of domestic violence or abuse. Sometimes, an accident may render a child an orphan.

When such misfortune strikes, family members come together and do what they must to make sure a child has the best possible chance for a good future. Gay men and lesbians are certainly not immune to such situations. Often they must accept the responsibility of caring for a child whose parents have died or been declared unfit, as in the case of Bryan.

Although their stories are very different, both Diane and Sarah became single parents because of situations beyond their control. When Diane's partner Patty became ill with breast cancer, the two women realized how important it was to plan for the future of Patty's son, Tony. Together, they decided that Diane should adopt Tony and become fully responsible for him in the eyes of the court. But it was frustrating that, unlike Wayne and Sal, Patty and Diane did not have the chance to win a case and set a precedent in their home state. Diane described what happened:

> [We] tried to do a second-parent adoption but we found out it was illegal in Kansas and we couldn't even do a precedent-setting case, in large part because Patty was dying. [Patty died on February 6, 1992.] It would be a moot point because one parent would be dead. We gave that up and in the end I was given guardianship of Tony before Patty died. Then after she died I immediately moved to adopt him.
>
> Luckily, the judge we had was an intelligent, open-mind-

ed individual. She was heterosexual but wasn't swayed by stereotypes. We had a social worker come and do a home visit. The court also appointed a *guardian ad litem* [a court-appointed guardian], an attorney who came and did another investigation. We worked very hard on showing these people that I had been Tony's mother just as much as Patty had been, taking care of him from the moment he was born. It would be an awful tragedy to take him away from the only other parent he ever knew.

I think one of the things that was so wonderful, that we did right, was being an out lesbian family. Because if we had been closeted, my rights and role in being Tony's parent wouldn't have been noticed. As an out family, everyone in town knew what I had done and that I had been there from the beginning.

Patty and I didn't talk about the legal arrangement at first because we were so busy raising this wonderful little boy. Having a baby is just really time consuming, and it seems that for the first year of his life, all we did was take care of him, be parents, work, and just get by. That's all we thought about in the beginning. We didn't start thinking about the legal aspects of our relationship until the Karen Thompson/Sharon Kowalski case and then [we] said we better look into this.[2] Of course, when Patty got sick, we knew we had to do something.

Right now the biggest thing is dealing with our grief and learning to be a family in our new configuration. We were a wonderful family before. We had a wonderful time together. We loved hanging out and playing and doing things.

We used to play baseball out in our front yard with a plastic ball and bat. It was just fun to be in this family. It was the best thing to ever happen to me. Now, I have to learn to be a single parent. The funny thing is, Patty and I used to laugh at how naive she was to think that alone she could raise a child. We were so glad, so smug that there were two of us.

Now I'm going to be a parent alone, I'm not so smug. I think the next year or so, or the next couple of years, will be spent learning this new way of being a family.

However they become parents, these lesbians and gay men are now most concerned with what's best for themselves and their children. The courage that Lynette and Julie, Wayne and Sal, Sarah, and Diane showed in standing before a court of law to petition to gain custody or adopt a child is something to admire. Nor was it easy for Joyce to defy convention and have her child alone, or for Jim and John to embrace their homosexuality after years of heterosexual marriage and the accompanying public approval. But even more impressive is the talent of all of these parents for creating strong, supportive families, no matter how they came to be.

3

OPENING
THE CLOSET
DOOR

There is a saying in the lesbian and gay community: "You don't choose to be gay, it chooses you." Whether or not this is true, learning to accept one's homosexual identity can be a long and arduous process. Once a person has come far enough to be comfortable identifying as gay or lesbian, he or she has begun the coming-out process.

The term "to come out" was coined about two decades ago and is rlated to the expression "hiding a skeleton in the closet." This meant that the family kept a scandalous secret hidden from friends or the public. Gay men or lesbians are often the "skeleton" families try to keep in the closet. Today, to "come out" refers to stepping outside of the closet to acknowledge your homosexuality—once thought to be shocking—to yourself or to others. Coming out of the closet is defying the notion that homosexuality is something to be hidden, that it is a shameful secret. There used to be no question about it: being gay or lesbian was a facet of one's personality to be concealed at all costs. Even today, some lesbians and gay men are thrown out of their homes and cut off from their families when their sexual orientation is revealed.

The initial coming out phase is a critical time because it requires facing some difficult questions. Is there something wrong with me? Will my family still love me? How will life be different? How will friends and family react to me? During this phase, one begins to separate the realities of life from what he or she was taught about how life should be lived. After deciding what fits, lesbians and gay men can begin making life choices that may be very different from those their parents made.

Coming out is a never-ending process, and one never does stop weighing its risks. Sometimes family members, friends, or coworkers feel that homosexuality is wrong. Some employers may decide that they don't want any lesbians or gay men working in their businesses and fire employees who acknowledge their sexual orientation.

Although some cities and counties have civil rights legislation that says a person may not be discriminated against because of sexual orientation, these rights are still often in jeopardy. Across the country, laws are being drafted to deny civil rights to gay men and lesbians. Most of these are found unconstitutional in the courts, but the threat of discrimination is always very near. In Colorado, voters passed a measure stating that there should be no antidiscrimination laws protecting the civil rights of lesbians and gay men.

Proponents of the measure see antidiscrimination ordinances as providing "special rights" to lesbians and gay men. Opponents of the Colorado measure say it denies a segment of the American population their rights. Even though voters passed this law, it has been challenged and will soon be considered by the U.S. Supreme Court.

Despite the difficulties with family, friends, or society, coming out can be an individual, liberating statement of pride that brings a renewed sense of self. Instead of hiding in a closet feeling isolated, lesbians and gays who are "out" (even if only to other lesbians and gays) can discover a large community of people to which they belong. A vocabulary, a network, a culture, and a history is suddenly theirs. Imagine a gathering where you are surrounded by hundreds or thousands of people who share the same feelings you do. Although the lesbian and gay community is as diverse as the rest of America, individuals feel strong bonds to each other based on their common goals and desires.

Some gay leaders are adamant in maintaining that coming out in the most public sense possible is the responsibility of every lesbian and gay man, especially those who are already in the public spotlight. They argue that actors, musicians, and elected officials must come out without regard to personal consequences. They claim that this will eradicate some of society's homophobia as people realize how many lesbians and gays they already know and like. Often cited as prime role models are U.S. Representative Barney Frank, actor Sir Ian MacKellen, singers k.d. lang and Melissa Etheridge, and tennis pro Martina Navratilova, who have all come out and continue to pursue successful careers. Others hold fast to the tenet that coming out is a very personal decision that can have very dangerous public ramifications. If you come out to a colleague, will word spread to your boss? Will it matter?

We never really know the circumstances and risks that permeate the lives of others. On a personal level, coming out means a great deal of individual liberation and fulfillment, yet it exacts a cost. There are difficulties associated with this kind of self-disclosure—not the least of which is the possibility of negative community reaction. Losing the love of a family member or a friend can be devastating.

For gay and lesbian parents, the price of coming out might be losing their children in a custody battle or being denied adoption rights. Often, the courts will refuse to recognize these men and women as good and lawful parents. This is a concern for most of the mothers and fathers in this book. Yet without hesitation, the parents who have come out agree that coming out was a good decision. They have been able to live affirming and honest lifestyles that include family, friends, intimate relationships, and, most importantly, their children. All seem to agree that the benefits far outweigh the drawbacks.

THE FIRST STEP

The first step out of the closet, which involves acknowledging one's homosexual feelings fully to oneself, can be a difficult one. Internalized homophobia is often at the heart of this struggle. An individual must grapple with societal expectations as well as her or his own intuitions and emotions. Internalized homophobia is the fear of homosexuality directed at oneself. Sometimes, this fear turns into self-hatred. But even then, soul-searching can help a person accept feelings and act on them in a positive and healthy manner.

For many gays and lesbians it takes years to successfully traverse this road. Others are able to acknowledge their homosexuality instinctively. Sarah, for instance, knew at a very young age.

In the sixth grade I had a bad crush on Tracy. I knew it was different—I lived and died to sleep at her house and eat dinner there. I knew that something was different. I wasn't really afraid of those feelings, but I knew that I should protect them and protect myself.

To know that there is something different about you and to know instinctively that you must hide it shows the power of the rules and roles society has assigned us. Sarah knew at a young age that sharing her feelings about Tracy would elicit negative reactions. While she didn't feel wrong about having these feelings, she knew others would judge them.

Jim and John also experienced homosexual feelings during their teen years, but instead of exploring them, they pushed them back and continued to lead the kind of lives that were expected of them. Jim says:

> I went through adolescence in the late fifties, early sixties in an Irish Catholic family. We sort of wrote the book on repression. I suppose I've known since the age of ten or twelve in one way or another that I'm gay. I fought it and fought the impulse successfully enough to finally get married in 1967.

John tells a similar story:

> Growing up, I knew there was something different and I knew there was an attraction difference. My feelings were different then. My reactions were different than my friends', but everything I'd heard about that sort of thing, no, it didn't interest me. What I wanted was to have a home and family and all the things everybody else seemed to want. That's what I pursued, and I certainly had a very active social life and dated women.

The circumstances of John's, Jim's, and Sarah's upbringings, as well as their community environments, greatly influenced their decisions about when to explore their emotions.

Coming Out to Family

Coming out to your spouse, your family, your friends, or your colleagues can be a scary undertaking. The fear of rejection from the people one loves is enough to make many people stay in the closet their whole lives. Others wait and watch and bide their time until they feel this disclosure will be well received.

Men and women who come out to family members often

strike some kind of compromise. Their parents must learn to overcome some of their own homophobia, and a new relationship must be forged. For each family this works differently. Sometimes acceptance is a long and painful process; sometimes it is quick and easy. But it is rarely without its share of heartache. When John eventually came out to his parents and siblings, no one seemed particularly interested, which left him wondering how close his "close-knit" family really was.

Joyce's brother and sisters easily accepted her lesbianism and her desire to have a son. She had a difficult time, however, coming out to her mother. When it became clear that she was having her baby as a single parent, tempers rose. Then her mother had to confront Joyce's lesbianism, and a period of denial ensued.

My mother thought I was insane. I walked into her house and I said, I just want you to know that I'm going to get pregnant. My mother said, "You're crazy. How could you want to do that?" And I said, "Well, I'm seeing a therapist, and she doesn't think I'm crazy, so I don't know why you should think I'm crazy. Do you want to see her with me?" My mother said, "Yes, because I want to meet someone that could be supportive of this sort of idea."

I had called her [the therapist] and said, "My mother's coming, and I just want you to be ready." [During the appointment] my mother's saying, "What kind of craziness is this that you could be supportive of her?" My therapist answered, "I know lots of single women who are pregnant." And then she said, "And I know lots of lesbians that are." And Mother goes, "Aha, that's what's going on here."

I hadn't come out to my parents, but I thought they knew. For ten years I had been with men. But Gail wasn't my first girlfriend. I just thought she [Mom] put two and two together.

The situation changed slightly when Joyce became pregnant.

> I never pretended I was married. My mother pretends I married. She pretends I met Frank [Michael's father], got pregnant, got married, and got divorced—all within eight months. She made it all up.

Jim had an easier time coming out to his extended family. He was able to build on a foundation of strong relationships developed over many years.

> It hasn't made any difference with my very conservative brother or his six children or my sister and her three kids. According to my brother, the reaction of one of my nephews when he read the letter in which I came out to my brother was that he shrugged and said, "Well, it won't make any difference. He's still Uncle Jim and he was always good to us kids." I think what made the difference in the reaction was that, both with my family and in the community here, I was an established figure. I was a known quantity. People had to decide whether or not they were going to be able to deal with this knowledge and whether or not they were going to be able to retain the friendship. I made it clear—not explicitly but in my behavior, I suppose—I wasn't going to consider this a change in my relationship with any of my friends. I was going to assume that the friendship would continue and it was up to them to show me that I was wrong. With that attitude, it turns out, I've lost none of my friends. And I've met a very interesting variety of brand new people.

How Far "Out" Is Okay?
There are varying degrees of being out and each person measures them differently. The line that distinguishes being in the closet is different for everyone. Many people are out to friends but not to their families. Others may be out to their

families but not at work. Still others may come out to individuals in specific circumstances that feel safe.

For Wayne, being out means no less than publicly acknowledging Sal as his life partner and Hope as their child. These two men made a conscious decision that they would adopt Hope as two loving partners who live as a family. This commitment to being out has made Wayne and Sal the first openly gay couple to adopt in the state of New York.

Although Joyce never sat down to discuss her lesbianism with her parents, she says she was never really in the closet. However, not everyone she comes in contact with knows that she is a lesbian. "I was never not out," she says. "I was never really closeted. I wasn't really out to everyone I knew. I'm still not out to everyone I know."

Julie and Lynette also make specific coming out choices based on where they live and what feels comfortable for them. Because of the pervasive homophobia that exists in their town, they have decided that coming out slowly and cautiously is the safest way. As the neighbors get to know their family better and friendships develop, their lesbianism will seem less important.

Both women now talk easily about the factors involved in determining how far "out" is okay.

> You just don't make difficult situations arise. We're out to certain people, we're out to the kids' doctors and those kinds of people. But we're not necessarily out to the neighbors who we don't usually see. But the people we deal with on a fairly regular basis, we're out to them. We concentrate on being the best people we can be and in having confidence in who we are.
>
> We live in a township outside of Ann Arbor and we live in the rural part of this township. It's a consolidated school system, primarily white, probably 50 percent working class and 50 percent middle class. It's not liberal.

Coming Out to the Children

Lesbian and gay parents think very carefully about when and how to come out to their children. Although waiting has the potential to cause difficulties, some people choose to wait until their children are older and may better understand. Deciding how and when to disclose one's homosexuality is always a complex process. Some children may resent the inherent dishonesty of a parent who continues a relationship with them without sharing such an important part of his or her life. On the other hand, perceptions and judgments about homosexuality may already be formed in the minds and hearts of some children, and homophobia may cause problems if the subject is broached.

Some lesbian and gay parents live their lives very openly with their children, and their same-sex relationship is not considered something out of the ordinary. Each parent's style is different, and timing and explanations must be carefully weighed.

Individual family circumstances also play an important role. For John, coming out to his children required much thought and planning. He had been married and had lived in "a nuclear family" for a long time. Telling his children that for much of that time, he was having feelings for men could have come as quite a shock and disappointment to them. John chose to wait until his daughter was in college and his son was in high school before coming out to them.

> I was intending to tell my son first, but my former wife called me one day and said, "Your daughter knows about you because she came to me this morning and said, 'I just want you to know that I'm pretty sure about Dad—that he's gay. When you get a chance, why don't you tell him that I know, so when he's comfortable, I'd like to talk to him about it.'"
>
> I broke the ice with my daughter, and I did it with a

joke I had heard about a year before. I simply said, "Do you know why life is tougher for a gay person than a black person?" She said, "No, why?" I said, "A black person never has to tell his family that he's black." Her eyes lit up and she said, "So are we going to talk about this?"

My son was a football player and I know that, just the type of person he is, if he had known about me [earlier] and any of his football friends would have said "fag," he would have smashed them around. I wanted to spare him from that. I didn't want him to be sensitive about me. I didn't want him to have to carry that while he was trying to make his own way. I knew he couldn't really understand it all and be totally comfortable. He'd just be kind of sensitive about it.

I lived in a place by myself and worked, went to ballgames, and did everything like anybody else. My kids knew they had a good dad, and I didn't want the town pitying them.

I waited for other reasons, too. When I finally left home, I had not accepted [being gay] yet. I accepted it as something that was, but I wasn't very happy with it because it had pretty much taken my life and split it all up. I had to start over again. I was not a happy person. I resented it, actually. And I didn't feel telling them from that type of viewpoint was a healthy thing. My children were just trying to find out who they were. What would happen when they learned that their father, who they thought was so secure, was just all screwed up. I didn't think that was real healthy.

Jim came out to his children when they were in high school, although he says he would have done it earlier if he had known at a younger age that he was gay. He notes that a homophobic remark was never allowed to go unchallenged in their home, and that this vigilance in teaching diversity paid off. He feels closer to his son and daughter than ever before.

The relationship with the kids is much better than it ever was. I'm not as distant from them. I'm not as removed from them as I was when I lived there.

The last few years that we were still [living] together, I would just avoid the family. If they were in the living room, I would be in the family room and vice versa. I would use office work as an excuse, or listening to music. They didn't share my taste in music, and I would use that as a way to stay away from them.

We talk to one another now.

For gay and lesbian parents who conceive children through alternative insemination or who adopt young children, coming out to kids can be molded into an educational strategy that teaches diversity and acceptance of different types of people.

Many parents, such as Diane or Wayne, feel their sexual orientation is a given. But teaching their children that their parents are good people even if society doesn't think so is a choice and a challenge. For all the parents in this book, coming out is an issue to approach with great forethought.

When Tony was born, Diane and her partner Patty were both active in local gay politics; but at such a young age, it did not seem odd to Tony to be raised by two women. At the time of Patty's death, Tony was old enough to begin asking some questions. Diane decided to wait to come out until Tony recovers from his mother's death and is ready for answers to his questions.

Among the parents in this book, methods of explaining their lifestyles and relationships differ. Some parents are concerned about the treatment a child will receive at school or from friends if they reveal their sexual orientation. It might open the door to some physical or emotional harm, as others might tease or taunt them.

Joyce is not in a hurry to explain everything to Michael

about homophobia and the ways society might view his mother.

> I don't even use the word lesbian to him. I'm getting ready to. I want him to be so intact in his identity and in who I am and who my friends are before he hears that some people don't think it's right. I don't hide anything. I sleep with my girlfriend here. He calls her my love person. He just doesn't have a name for the lifestyle.

Sarah describes a time when Bryan was only three or four years old, and he was already questioning why she and her then partner couldn't participate in marriage rituals.

> He said something about we couldn't have a honeymoon because how could we be married. Yet he wanted us to have that honeymoon. He wanted that union spirit. But somehow in his brain, it didn't quite fit the puzzle.
>
> I explained to Bryan that people have different kinds of relationships. There're different kinds of families. We went to a rehearsal a couple of years ago at the gay men's chorus and we left there and he said to me, "Are all those men lesbians?" I said, "No, they're gay." He said, "Does that mean they're like lesbians?" I said, "Yes, but they have relationships with men."
>
> Then he said that they couldn't do that. I tried to explain, "Is it okay for me to love Nancy?" I tried to make that relationship with him, and he sort of mused. He wasn't repulsed or grossed out about it, but he's not sure this fits what society tells him.
>
> In his first-grade class, only 4 percent of the kids came from intact heterosexual families. The divorce rate and family dysfunction have bred a situation where kids really do come from different families and it's not just *Heather Has Two Mommies*.[1] That has helped him not feel like he's an

alien or something because he has a lesbian mom. He understands two women love each other or two men love each other. He's very comfortable with that.

It will be interesting to me when he's eleven and twelve and kids start to harass him—how he defends himself. I hope that he's comfortable enough with it to stand up to it. Because certainly I know that will happen.

Lynette and Julie often review coming out issues within the family. They value open discussion and spend time explaining again and again why, how, and to whom to come out.

The kids were seven, three, and four when we got them. We always explained it as our relationship, and as they get older they have more questions. It bothers them a little more now than it used to because of peer pressure, and they're more aware.

The family often holds meetings during which Julie and Lynette say they "talk about differences, caring, loving, sharing. We talk about choosing who to tell; which friends can be trusted and which friends can't. We talk about making the decision to tell people based on some kind of halfway specific relationship as opposed to just telling someone you run into that your parents are gay."

Schools, Neighbors, and the Cub Scouts
Almost every day presents an opportunity for a lesbian or gay parent to come out. Interactions with doctors, teachers, neighbors, and parents of kids' friends force a parent to decide whether or not it is safe and appropriate to share her or his sexual orientation. John chose not to come out to neighbors and friends. He and his wife lived in the same small town where they had both grown up, and their two children were still in school. He explains:

I took a job in Chicago and, at the time, I was the president of the local school board. We were all involved in church activities, and everybody in town knew everything about us, except this. We told everyone that this was a career opportunity, and that I was going to give it a year before I packed my family up and moved them around. Everybody bought it, of course. We even handled the divorce in Chicago. In fact, it was probably another year or year and a half before most of the community even realized that we were divorced.

Somehow, during the next couple of years, we got wind of some gossip in the town about my sexuality. I was very quiet about it, so it was all speculation. I simply contacted those people, visited their homes, and told them that I had understood they had a problem or a question about my sexuality. I was there if they wanted to ask me about it. I really didn't tell them anything. I didn't tell them yes or no. But I certainly left there giving them the impression that I was not.

Among my own family there was a lot of chitchat. They had a feeling like everybody else did. I approached all of them but they didn't want to talk to me about it.

Julie and Lynette use their instincts when deciding who to tell. Even before the adoption was completed, they had decided that the children would call them "Mom" and "Julie" for very specific reasons.

If they're calling both of us Mom then that means people will automatically know [our sexual orientation]. We didn't want to force the kids to be out all of the time. Because Julie and I are not out [in every situation]. At first I didn't know how I'd feel, and I didn't know how the kids would feel. I didn't feel comfortable having those choices made for them. Right now, they can choose to tell people if they want to.

69

Some parents have chosen to circumvent these decisions by being out in a very public sense. Sal and Wayne have Hope call them Daddy Sal and Daddy Wayne. They are very involved in school and community activities and keep in close contact with Hope's teachers. Sarah, however, feels the need to remain prudent regarding her interactions with Bryan's teachers and other parents. Although she is concerned about making sure that educators know about Bryan's past physical abuse, she is also keenly aware of the problems that could arise should homophobia cloud the schoolroom or a scout meeting. Sarah doesn't make a point of coming out to teachers, but she says, "Bryan's teachers know about his abusive situation. I don't walk in and say I'm a lesbian parent. Certainly, it's obvious I'm a single parent."

But others in Sarah's circle have "figured it out." In fact, she tells of a gratifying situation in which nothing explicit was said, but suddenly all was understood.

> Most of Bryan's closest friends at school [and] most of their parents have figured out that I'm a lesbian. At a Cub Scout meeting that spring, right after the March on Washington [for Gay and Lesbian Rights], I drove home all day to take Bryan to Cub Scouts. I'm sitting in Cub Scouts having total culture shock. Here I have just spent the weekend with a million gay and lesbian people in a very affirming atmosphere, and I come home and the very first thing I have to do is take my then eight-year-old son to Cub Scouts. The woman sitting next to me, the parent of a friend of Bryan's whom I know and we take care of each other's kids, turned to me and said, "Did you go?" I said, "Go where?" She said, "Didn't you go to the march? Wasn't it great?"
>
> You know, after I got over my initial shock, we had a wonderful conversation about it. Then I imagined that Marilyn probably had been waiting two years to find the time and the place to say, "Hey, it's okay." Then I found out that her ex-husband had AIDS and just passed away. It's

been very affirming for me to talk about it—have it be out. But, it's still scary.

Coming out is an act that is repeated over and over again every time the information is shared with a new friend, another coworker, or even one's physician. Sometimes the decision is spontaneous. Sometimes it is planned and agonized over for weeks, months, or even years. Whatever the situation, it is an affirmation of identity.

Periods of coming out are also important times for the friend, colleague, or family member who shares one's life. Jim says that in three years of coming out, he has never had a negative response. In fact, he cites a surprising experience while on a business trip away from the comfortable surroundings of home.

> I was at a convention in San Diego and ended up coming out to a businesswoman, her husband, and a client of hers in a conversation over dinner about gays in the military. When they left the restaurant, the reaction of one of the businessmen was to come back to my table and thank me because he had learned something that night during our discussion. I was just flabbergasted.

Perhaps it is Jim's maturity, his demeanor, or his ease in sharing his sexual orientation that has won him such positive reactions. Or it may be his honesty and willingness to share that elicits good responses from others.

> I guess through coming out I realized that I'm very sure of myself. For years, I didn't think I was. For years, I felt very unsure of myself, despite the evidence around me. It [coming out] made a difference in my life.

4

FAMILY LIFE

Hope has two daddies to make her lunch and drive her to school. Michael stays with his grandparents several afternoons a week. Keem, Quan, and David have sleep-over parties and go to Girl Scouts meetings where Mom is the troop leader.

What's it like to live in a family headed by lesbians or gay men? Ask a child living in one of them and she'll probably tell you it's much like living in any other family. Except in their families, there might be two mommies or two daddies, but rarely one of each.

The aspects of gay and lesbian families that differ from traditional families are noticed less in what happens in the home than what happens out in public. While children of lesbians and gays may not think their lives are so very different from those of their friends, the outside world may think so. Issues of when and to whom to come out arise daily, and children must be prepared to handle possible taunts from classmates.

But for all of the differences, there are many similarities between families—gay or straight. It's their individual identities that make them original and endearing. Because some of the traditional definitions of family don't fit gay and lesbian families they often enjoy a greater amount of freedom when it comes to experimenting with new lifestyles and inventing unique family traditions. Often this means that the definition of who a family member is becomes enlarged. Friends may be considered part of the family and share holiday dinners or weekend outings. Or certain holidays may have a slightly different meaning for children such as Hope who know to make two cards in school for Father's Day rather than just one. Sometimes, the family is involved in social or political organizations that focus on gay men, lesbians, and their families. For instance, John's two children were active with him in the Gay and Lesbian Parents Coalition International, an organization that acts as a link for local groups that provide support, education, and social opportunities for lesbian and gay families.

FAMILIES OF AFFINITY

Families of affinity, or families created through bonds of love and support, is the term that best describes gay and lesbian families. They are unique in their structure, their daily routines, and in their development of rules and order.

For example, Michael has known from a very early age who the key adults are in his life. Joyce is Mom. She's the one who will give permission to go play or to buy a new toy. After school Michael gets the chance to spend time with some of the other adults in his life. Frank, Michael's biological father, picks him up from school on Mondays and Tuesdays. Sometimes they'll do something special, or sometimes they'll just spend time together talking. Although he is only eight years old, Michael understands that his father donated the sperm necessary to make him—but that Mom is the one who signs report cards and has the final say on any matter. At home, Michael knows he'll find either his mom or Gail.

Sometimes, Michael will head for his grandparents' home,

the same house where Joyce grew up. He has his own set of dresser drawers, and his voice is even on the phone-answering machine. He knows Mom will pick him up on her way home from work.

The male and female adults who help care for Michael don't create confusion for him. Instead they provide a warm, loving extended family of which Michael is a treasured member. For a working mother such as Joyce, this arrangement makes perfect sense.

Joyce considers herself a single parent, but she's created a family unit that provides her with a lot of help. The family configuration combines her biological family, her ex-lover, and the biological father. Because Gail was Joyce's partner when Michael was an infant and even took part in the insemination and the birth, Michael has grown up identifying Gail as a parent. Today, even though Joyce and Gail are no longer romantically connected, they still share the same house and many of the responsibilities of raising Michael. "He knows relationships move and change, but he knows Gail will never leave him and that I'll never leave him," explains Joyce. "We're his parents, and we'll always take care of him. Gail and I pretty much split everything. Nothing is written and nothing is organized. We just do it. I like that, and I know that we'll be a family forever."

This unique family unit includes the very active participation of Joyce's parents, who relish their roles as baby-sitters and daytime caregivers. Joyce says, "They've always done the child care for him. Between me and Gail working, they've always taken care of him. He's the apple of their eye." She continues:

> He sees his family as me, Gail, and him. Then he sees my family as his family, a blood relative family that includes my whole extended family. He feels very attached. Michael calls Gail's mother and sisters Grandma and Auntie. While he

considers them part of his family, Michael sees them much less often.

Wayne and Sal's daughter, Hope, also feels attached to her extended family. As a baby, she was practically abandoned and spent her first few months of life battling disease. Even though her skin is a different color than her father's, she now has a permanent home and an extended family—including grandparents—who love her dearly. Family activities and involvement in their daughter's life is very important, says Wayne.

> Sal and I were very active in the parents group that was in the preschool. All of the kids and teachers in her classes knew about Daddy Wayne and Daddy Sal; our pictures were up on the board like everybody else's. We were intimately involved. She's in public school now. The teachers have been wonderful. The principal's been wonderful, partly due to the fact that we are very upfront about everything and we approach it immediately. I don't want anything to happen to my daughter because of something that I'm doing, or because of us.
>
> We introduce ourselves as gay parents and we inform them of [her adoption] and how she relates to us. A big concern to us is what everybody does around Mother's Day because she doesn't have anybody. We make sure that they focus on her grandmother. On Father's Day she needs to be allowed to make two things, not one, which is usually no problem for anybody. But we're real upfront about it. We're active in the Parent's Association, we're active fund-raisers, we're known.
>
> We believe very strongly that by not ranting and raving but by demonstrating positive images and being role models that we're accepted. My concern about my child's education is just that of anybody else's. The rest of the par-

ents of the kids in her class see that. [Hope] has had no has-
sles up to now, but we're very early in her educational career.

Hope is dramatically aware of the fact that she's in a
nontraditional household. She's very aware that she has two
daddies. She knows lots of gay and lesbian parents so it's a
normal occurrence to her, but she also knows that she's the
only one in her classroom.

My role as a parent is to give her a warm, loving, nurturing environment, to let her grow up to meet her full
potential. That's any parent's role. There's no difference if
you're lesbian or gay. Sal and I hope that we can build in
her a strength of character that when someday, and it's
inevitable, someone comes up to her in the schoolyard and
says, "Your daddy's a faggot," she can turn around and say,
"So, what," and walk away.

WHAT MAKES A FAMILY WORK?

Extending family structures beyond the nuclear definition is
nothing new. In many cultures, generations of mothers and
fathers and grandparents and children live and work together. In developing a culture of lesbian and gay families, similar
setups exist which include friends, lovers past and present,
and in many cases, blood relatives. Some of the parents interviewed for this book, such as Wayne and Sal or Julie and
Lynette, have been able to divide responsibilities and coor-
dinate schedules between them. In each family, both parents
are involved in parent-teacher conferences, after-school activities, and running the household.

But for single parents such as Sarah or Diane, there are
a few extra complications and challenges, because all of the
responsibility for raising their children rests on their shoulders
alone. Diane explains how much fun it was to be a family
when her life partner Patty was alive. And both shared so
much of the work that Diane was able to enjoy her role as
coparent without feeling overwhelmed.

We worked real hard on doing "halfies" and taking turns. It was real important to both of us. I remember a childhood where my father vanished and my mother did everything, and she went nuts. My father had no connection to us. Patty and I very much wanted to take turns getting up in the middle of the night or doing the different things that had to be done.

Now that Diane is a single parent, her concept of family has changed to include a number of close friends who pitch in and help her handle the strains of raising a child and running her own business.

Sarah, too, has little help in raising Bryan. But her commitment to him knows no bounds. She admits to changing her social patterns to revolve more around Bryan. As he grows older though, she's aware that he will need her around less and less.

He's in school and he has a life of his own. He wants to do things. He's much more demanding but in a good way. I have had to shift. I've had to make room for my parental responsibilities. I'm a member of the PTA and the Cub Scouts, and I'm available to take him and friends to movies.

Sarah has also made allowances for the intimate relationships in her life.

The last woman I was involved with had a challenging time dealing with the fact that I was a parent. I wasn't able to be totally spontaneous and get up and go. "No, I've got to get a sitter," or, "No, Bryan and I have plans." There wasn't a lot of equality because I had parenting responsibilities.

It is vital for Bryan to know that his mom will always be there for him, even if she begins dating someone. "Just because I'm involved with somebody doesn't mean he's going to automatically get a second parent," says Sarah. "I'm the anchor. I'm the parent. That was an adjustment for me because I've always wanted to have a marriage-type relationship with a woman where we have a union and we're bonded and have a commitment ceremony and the whole ball of wax. When I got Bryan, that desire intensified. I wanted my family unit. But I've had to accept that my primary role and function is a parent."

Sarah is also struggling with finding more male role models for Bryan. This is a concern for some parents, but very often, men or women automatically enter into their lives and develop meaningful relationships with their children. For example, Wayne says that he and Sal have close women friends who have taken a great interest in Hope. He looks forward to them playing a larger role in Hope's life in the years to come.

Sarah acknowledges that Bryan has men in his life—teachers at school, the men in her gay synagogue, and fathers of his friends. But he's made it clear that he wants a big brother. Sarah explains, "I'm thinking of finding one for him through one of these Big Brother programs. I'd love to do it through a structured program, [but] I don't want to have to screen for a lesbian-sensitive figure. I don't want to have to, at the same time that I'm Bryan's mom, be educating a straight family or a straight man about what it means to be gay or lesbian."

FAMILIES BORN OF DIVORCE

When established families are forced to change because a parent comes out as gay or lesbian, unconventional structures emerge. Suddenly, family traditions that were taken for granted have to be reformatted. This is similar to what happens when two heterosexual parents get divorced. Who spends which holidays with whom? Where? Who else besides the blood relatives are invited?

These questions all get answered eventually, although sometimes it may take some time for new patterns and new traditions to emerge.

John and his ex-wife dealt with many of these questions after he came out as a gay man and moved out of the family home. After getting his divorce, he continued to spend holidays with his ex-wife and children.

> About the first four years, we still had our Christmas mornings. I would pack up things and drive down there about five in the morning. We'd put everything up, we had coffee, and we had our Christmas. The kids wanted it. They asked if we would do it, and neither one of us had an objection. That was their little fantasy that they wanted to have once a year and that was fine. I felt like they deserved that, and certainly we enjoyed it, too. We did that until the Christmas before my ex-wife remarried.

LABELS—DEFINING ROLES

The names Daddy Wayne and Daddy Sal have been a part of Hope's lexicon since she joined their family. Even at two years old she couldn't be swayed by the court-appointed lawyer who said she couldn't have two daddies. To Hope, it didn't matter who was the legal parent or which one made her lunch; they were equal in her eyes.

Because the traditional names Mother and Father aren't exact fits for lesbian and gay parents, deciding what they should be called can be a tricky business. The chosen terms can strongly affect the life of a family, because so much of our daily existence is defined by words. Mother and Father, for example, connote very separate meanings in American society. The lawyer who came to question Hope was so controlled by labels, words, and tradition, he felt sure no child could have two fathers.

What happens when the gender of the parents doesn't

match traditional descriptions? The answer is different for every lesbian and gay family. Some parents recognize the effect using certain labels will have on their child's development and plan ahead to determine what the child will call them, as well as how they will be introduced to neighbors, principals, or doctors. Other parents let nature take its course, knowing that nicknames and pet names so often emerge unplanned.

Lynette and Julie decided what Keem, David, and Quan would call them even before the adoption had been approved. They had to consider the implications of their children having two "mothers" in a small town where lesbianism is not acceptable. Lynette is "Mom" and Julie is "Julie." All lesbian and gay parents must take into account what their community will interpret from the names their children use to address them. In some cases, it is preferable that a child call each parent "Mother" or "Mom," whereas in Julie and Lynette's case, there is clearly some risk involved.

For others, being called "Mom" means a great deal. For several years after Bryan had been living with her, Sarah's relationship to Bryan had been emotionally defined, but their last names remained different. At his request, Bryan's last name was changed to match Sarah's, and when the two are together, calls of "Mom" fill the air.

5

HARSH LEGALITIES— FIGHTING FOR EQUAL RIGHTS

After deciding to have a baby, Joyce made a conscious choice to keep her affairs out of the legal system. She explains that there were no contracts drawn up between her and Frank nor partnership agreements made between her and Gail: "I didn't want anything written down. I still have nothing written down. I don't want to have to deal with the legal system. It's a mess."

Lynette and Julie are both professionals working in the field of child welfare so they were knowledgeable about the legal requirements pertaining to adoption. Their familiarity with the adoption process proved very beneficial. For instance, they knew that the state courts did not look favorably on gay or lesbian adoptions. Their proceedings went smoothly, but only because of some difficult choices made by the two women. For one thing, they had to play it safe and not disclose their sexual orientations, indeed the very essence of their relationship, because they feared that the state would not grant custody to two lesbians. The two women are glad that they never said that they were lesbians. But they admit that no one was fooled. Legally, Lynette is the parent. As Julie explains:

> At the time, the courts hadn't become as flexible as they have become recently. Because Lynette was an administrator of a public agency, we had to have another agency do the home study. The social worker, probably in about twenty minutes, realized what the deal was. But knowing the political arena and because of Lynette's position, we had to say no [about being lesbian]. The caseworker said, "Okay, I can understand," and she went through it as she was supposed to have gone through it. She would come and visit, and do interviews.
>
> Then she said, "It will be okay."
>
> The only thing that happened at court was in the middle of the hearing the judge said, "Who is Julie?" I just said, "That's me, your honor." And that was it. She kind of nodded her head knowingly and completed the adoption.

It is a confusing web of silent nuances, legal strategies, and personal interpretations of unclear laws in which lesbians and gay men must navigate whenever they find themselves dealing with America's legal system. Until recently, there were no laws protecting gay men and lesbians. Both individuals and the courts were free to discriminate against them, and there was little recourse for these victims. Fortunately, the current climate is improving because of the tireless efforts of gay men, lesbians, and straight people who have been fighting such inequities for more than a quarter of a century.

AN HISTORICAL PERSPECTIVE

In 1969, a rebellion broke out against the police at the Stonewall Inn, a gay bar in New York's Greenwich Village. For the first time, gay men, lesbians, and transvestites (men in women's clothing) fought back when the police came—yet again—to raid the bar. This ground-breaking revolt etched itself in the annals of lesbian and gay history, and today it stands as a foremost symbol of lesbian and gay activism. The riot, which lasted days, signaled a new self-awareness for homosexuals: the realization that they shouldn't have to endure daily harassment and second-class status. A civil-rights movement was born.

Initially, the activist groups that developed after Stonewall were concerned primarily with such basic civil-rights issues as the right not to be fired from a job or evicted from an apartment because of sexual orientation. But as their leaders began learning more about the political process, they realized the magnitude of their task.

One of the first groups formed after the riots was the Gay Liberation Front where the ideas of "gay power" and equal rights were voiced. But there were other groups that had formed before the riots such as the Mattachine Society and the Daughters of Bilitis (D.O.B.). In 1948, a man named Henry Hay started the Mattachine Society, which concerned itself with fighting for the rights of homosexual men. The Daughters of Bilitis was started in 1955 by a lesbian couple, Del Martin and Phyllis Lyon, first as a social group. It soon began to fight for legal rights and published a magazine called *The Ladder*. *The Ladder* was an important "underground" magazine for lesbians in the 1950s and 1960s. It included a mix of literary articles and features about legal struggles facing lesbians.[1]

In general, lesbians and gay men began to heighten their visibility with organizations focusing on local issues and later on national issues. In San Francisco in 1971, the Alice B. Toklas Memorial Democratic Club (named after the writer Gertrude Stein's lesbian partner) was formed. It quickly became active in registering gay men to vote and in working with politicians seeking public office. Two years later the

National Gay Task Force was formed to fight for gay rights. (It later changed its name to the National Gay and Lesbian Task Force.) This organization has grown to become an important political organization involved in national discussions of issues such as gays in the military and the rights of lesbian and gay families.

Just as the Stonewall riots spurred people to action, the notorious Florida orange juice spokesperson, Anita Bryant, galvanized gay men and lesbians across the country when she began to publicy denounce homosexuals. In the 1970s Bryant, a popular "all-American" figure, received a great deal of national attention and public support in her campaign to deny equal rights to lesbians and gay men. In response to Bryant's public rallies and grassroots organizing, organizations such as the National Gay Task Force became active and a number of gay men and lesbians around the country stood up to be counted. Eventually, Bryant was silenced but not before she succeeded in stirring the pot by letting subtle and overt agents of discrimination float to the top.

Although change had begun, gays and lesbians continued to face blatant homophobia throughout the seventies. On television and in the movies, gay men often appeared as stereotypically effeminate and lesbians weren't shown at all. Several states had sodomy laws on the books that continued to outlaw consensual oral-to-genital or anal-to-genital sexual relations. While these laws applied to heterosexuals as well, they were only trotted out for cases involving gays and lesbians. During this period the courts routinely denied child custody to mothers who were proved or rumored to be homosexual.

While all these controversies were surfacing, gays and lesbians began forming arguments for equality and learning the tactics of activism and the formulas for fomenting social change. The Alice B. Toklas Memorial Democratic Club understood the importance of gay men voting in elections, and the

D.O.B. recognized the power of communicating news and ideas to lesbians through its magazine. The progress of today's gay and lesbian organizations owes much to the foundation created by those groups active in the 1950s, 1960s, and 1970s.

These efforts were always hindered, however, by the millions of lesbians and gay men who were not "out of the closet" because they feared for their jobs as well as their reputations, and didn't want to be rejected by those they loved. The contradiction of fighting for one's rights without coming out created difficulties. By staying invisible, closeted gay men and lesbians made it almost impossible to estimate how many people were directly affected by these issues. Invisibility also made it difficult for average Americans to relate to the fight because they knew no openly lesbian women or gay men.

The eighties brought greater change. The AIDS epidemic hit, and the gay and lesbian community was forced to reapportion its resources and its focus. Being sick with an illness that was only associated with gay men left many of those afflicted no choice but to come out. Weakened and sick with a disease that had not yet turned on the straight population, these men began sharing their secrets and turning to their families and straight friends for care, compassion, and comfort. People were dying, and it no longer seemed as important to stay in the closet when there was so much work to do and so many lives to be saved.

Gay and lesbian community leaders responded to the AIDS crisis with a still somewhat limited knowledge of the ins and outs of politics and organizing on a large scale. But fundraising and nonprofit management skills were quickly sharpened, and the battle to educate people about the disease took on the utmost importance. Discrimination against gay men (especially those who were perceived to have HIV or AIDS) was rising, and community leaders realized the need to continue with the original task of securing equal rights.

Discrimination affects everyone, whether or not he or she is a member of the targeted group. Many lesbians and gay men felt that if people with AIDS were discriminated against so easily and with such little resistance, discrimination against sexual orientation itself would also remain acceptable. Discrimination against lesbian mothers was still blatant in the courts. Divorced lesbian mothers lived in fear, because with one angry word from a spouse or family member, a judge could easily take away their children.

The need to fight such discrimination was heightened during this period when Ronald Reagan's presidential administration refused to grant money or resources to the AIDS fight, thereby further marginalizing the gay community and those with the disease. Public figures incited people's fear and ignorance. The Reverend Jerry Falwell once told a group of followers that "AIDS is the 'judgement of God.'"[2]

In the early 1980s during the early days of the AIDS epidemic, there was, as yet, no significant nationally organized movement to fight AIDS and combat such behavior. Instead, smaller organizations sprouted across the country to meet a variety of needs. Some focused on health and basic assistance, such as the Gay Men's Health Crisis (GMHC) in New York City. Others leaned more toward providing emotional support, such as Horizons Community Services and Howard Brown Memorial Clinic in Chicago. Later in the epidemic, militant groups like ACT UP (AIDS Coalition to Unleash Power) used public displays of anger and defiance— sit-ins, kiss-ins, die-ins, rallies, and public protests—to gain publicity for the fight against the disease. These actions complemented other efforts such as those of the National Gay and Lesbian Task Force, which chose to work within the system and focused on educating and lobbying legislators. Public marches such as the first "National March on Washington for Lesbian and Gay Rights" in 1979 demonstrated the power of numbers. More than 100,000 people marched. The second march in 1987 drew 500,000 and the third in 1993 drew more than 1 million.

Although there was no one philosophy to which all groups subscribed and disagreements arose as to methods, the variety of activities proved a good mix. Businesses and politicans learned that if they didn't work with the gay and lesbian political and social organizations, they would soon be picketed by ACT UP and subjected to unpleasant publicity. A 1989 march in Austin, Texas, saw thirty thousand people demanding more funding for AIDS programs and a repeal of the state's sodomy laws. The next day, members of ACT UP wrapped red tape around the state capitol to illustrate their frustration with the bureaucracy surrounding AIDS efforts.[3]

This lesson was learned again by the state of Colorado in 1993 when voters tried to repeal gay rights laws. A national boycott hurt the state financially when several large conventions scheduled to be held in Colorado were moved to different states and vacationers chose other locations.

By the time AIDS was finally recognized as a national crisis and not just one limited to gay men, the gay and lesbian community had matured in its political activism and raised the level of the social services it provided to its own.

Twenty-five years after Stonewall and more than a decade after the AIDS epidemic began, family issues have become a central focus for the community now that so much progress for gay and lesbian rights has been made. Gay and lesbian lawyers, activists, and parents across the country are using their talents to obtain adoption and foster-parenting rights, to legalize same-sex adoptions, and to pass domestic partnerships laws.

Domestic partnership laws were designed to offer benefits to unmarried couples that would equal those of married couples. Few of us may realize the legal and financial benefits that are conferred upon any man and woman who share a marriage license. They need not live together, care for each other, or have children to exercise these rights. A marriage license means not only legal status and societal approval, but it also grants tax advantages, inheritance preferences, hospital visiting rights, and the right for both partners to adopt the same child. But same-sex couples who do live together, care for one another, share financial burdens, and raise children together are not protected by strong domestic partnership rights, so they cannot take advantage of these marital privileges.

Diane found out how unfair the laws are when Patty died. Diane was quick to initiate adoption proceedings for Tony, and she expected some difficulties. However, she hadn't counted on being subjected to financial penalties for what she inherited from Patty. She and Patty had combined their finances as any couple would, but legally they could only be considered friends. Diane explains:

> People need to understand that lesbian and gay families have almost no rights. For example, I had to pay inheritance tax on our community property and, I'm working right now to not have to pay inheritance tax on my own income.
>
> We had joint bank accounts just like any couple, and we bought cars together. We did everything together, because we are a family. My attorney and my accountant found out that I had to pay tax on whatever Patty had given me.
>
> Even though we had bought the car together, she had to be considered half owner of the car, and I had to pay tax on her half.
>
> In a heterosexual marriage, the car would be considered community property. Anything you buy together in a heterosexual marriage is community property. A widow doesn't pay tax on the car she bought with her husband because they bought it together. But because we're not a family, legally, I have to pay tax on all of our community

property. I filed the return nine months after Patty died, sent in a check for about $2,500, leaving us a little bit uncertain financially. I've gotten a reply back from the inheritance section telling me that I have to prove the amount of money I put into the joint bank account. Everything that I did [or bought] I have to prove that I own half of it or I have to pay [inheritance] tax on my own income.

The interesting thing is that through this process I've gotten to know the vice president at the bank, and he's become a gay rights advocate. He said, "Boy, I really understand what you're going through. This isn't fair, maybe the legislature should change these laws."

Indeed, the laws are changing. To understand a discussion of parental rights, one must first understand the legalities of what it means to be a "legal" family, and the struggle to establish domestic partnerships.

STATE OF THE UNION

Medical technology has coincided with a new awakening about parenting. Lesbians and gay men are having and raising children in record numbers. But they are doing it without the same legal protection afforded their heterosexual counterparts. Using the U.S. Census Bureau definition of family, "a group of two or more persons related by birth, marriage, or adoption and residing together in a household,"[4] one might assume that lesbian and gay families simply do not exist. There is no mention or allowance for any broader definition that might offer them a place.

To provide some sort of legal status to nonmarried couples of all types, "domestic partnership" ordinances have been drafted and adopted in San Francisco, New York City, and about 15 municipalities across the country.[5] This trend holds many promises for lesbian and gay couples. In its purest sense, domestic partnership would give homosexual families the same rights and privileges enjoyed by heterosexual families. The problem, however, is that each ordinance defines domestic partnership differently and each grants different rights. San Francisco's ordinance, for example, recognizes domestic partnerships as families by defining them as, "two people who have chosen to share one another's lives in an intimate and committed relationship of mutual care."[6] Other ordinances require partners to be financially responsible for one another, or they specify a minimum length of time that the couple have to be together before they are entitled to coverage.

The majority of ordinances are quite limited and most assure equal medical benefits and bereavement leave only to the partners of city employees. Businesses and insurance companies are still free to discriminate.

But these are local laws. On a federal level, same-sex couples are not afforded benefits such as those under the Family Medical Leave Act. The federal Family Medical Leave Act mandates that a man or woman may take several weeks off of work to care for a legal spouse, child, or other family member and then return to the same job he or she left. Under this law, a lesbian could not stay home from work to care for her partner no matter how long they had been a couple.

Some cities, such as New York City, offer a domestic partnership registry in which couples can pay a small fee to have their names listed. Unfortunately, this is a mostly symbolic act, as it guarantees no other benefits to those who are not city employees.

Ironically, it is the world of big business that is moving fastest toward granting gay and lesbian employees equal benefits. The Lotus Development Corporation, a computer software company, was one of the first to offer the partners of gay and lesbian employees medical coverage and other benefits equal to those heterosexual spouses have had for years. Many other companies, large and small, are following suit as they are able to overcome their concerns about rising costs with pos-

LESBIAN AND GAY PROGRESS

The lesbian and gay community can count a number of important achievements towards the fight for equal rights and societal tolerance. These include:

- Anti-discrimination ordinances prohibiting discrimination because of sexual orientation are in effect in some cities. These laws make it illegal to fire an employee or refuse service to someone perceived to be lesbian or gay.
- There are openly gay and lesbian officials at several levels of government. Congressman Barney Frank and former congressman Garry Studds, both openly gay men, served in the U.S. House of Representatives. Roberta Achtenburg was appointed by President Clinton to be the undersecretary of housing and urban development despite Senator Jesse Helms's proclamation that she was a "damn lesbian." A sitting judge in Illinois is an openly gay man, and in 1994 the first black lesbian was appointed to the federal appeals court.
- Books and movies are beginning to show sympathetic and nonstereotypical gay men and lesbians. In 1994 actor Tom Hanks won an Academy Award for his performance as a gay man with AIDS in the movie *Philadelphia*. Lesbian and gay authors such as Paul Monette, Adrienne Rich, Edmund White, and Audre Lorde have been recognized with literary awards and heightened book sales.
- Newspapers have recognized the number of readers who are homosexual. Deb Price, a lesbian, became the first to have a syndicated column in mainstream newspapers in which she discusses gay and lesbian issues as well as other life issues.

itive results and limited, if any, additional financial burdens. Any extra costs are often justified by increased employee productivity and loyalty.

Moral issues have presented the most difficult barriers for lesbian and gay couples. Marriage is not only a legal institution, it also has religious roots that are woven into the fabric of American life. Conventional weddings are conducted by ministers, priests, and rabbis, according to the laws of each religion. Such traditions carry over into secular America, including the idea that marriage is a holy union between a man and a woman designed to bring children into the world. Even if one is not a particularly religious person, American culture is filled with religious influences. For instance, the national anthem contains the words, "one nation under God," and sessions of the U.S. Congress are opened with a nondenominational prayer.

Religious institutions can also be very powerful politically. At the 1992 Republican National Convention, the so-called "Religious Right," a broad term referring to a large number of vocal conservative Christian organizations, dominated the proceedings with talk of traditional family values and attitudes of blatant homophobia. America watched Pat Buchanan and others condemn and defame homosexuals on television before millions of viewers. Their words are matched by action. Members of conservative religious organizations are winning seats on school boards and in local governments on platforms of homophobia and intolerance.

What does this mean for gay and lesbian parents? For Diane, it means that she and Tony (along with the rest of her town) must deal with the antics of extremist Fred Phelps, a self-proclaimed minister. Phelps is famous for picketing the funerals of gay men and those who have died from AIDS. He and his family march holding signs that read "FAGS DESERVE TO DIE," or "AIDS IS GOD'S PUNISHMENT."

Diane explains that, as an activist, she is working to

counter the harmful effects of men such as Phelps. But when doing so, she is careful to leave Tony safely in the care of friends. "When there's a march I don't take him with me because I don't want him to have to see that stuff . . . when the hate people are there. I don't think it's time for him to have to march up the street and have people screaming at him and at his mother. I know someday he'll have to face it, and I know that it's going to be hard."

CAUTION AND COMPROMISE

Legal advances and the activism of people such as Diane have had a profound impact on the lesbian and gay civil rights movement. However, much still depends on state and local laws—as Julie and Lynette could tell you. Even in a gay/lesbian supportive environment, caution and compromise are what it takes to successfully adopt a child.

When Wayne and Sal decided to approach Hope's adoption as a gay couple, they had the intention of paving the road for others to follow. They succeeded in becoming the first openly gay couple to legally adopt a child in the state of New York. The process was a long and difficult one that had the potential of setting an important precedent. However, because of the personal beliefs of one man associated with the case, Wayne and Sal's efforts will not have the far-reaching impact they envisioned. Although Wayne is angry about this, he admits that what they did was first and foremost done with Hope in mind. After the petition for adoption, another year passed before Hope was legally their daughter. Wayne explains:

> When we approached the court for the adoption, there was nothing being hidden in any way. The judge in our case made us do a couple of things that he probably would not have done to nongay families. I was annoyed when it was

happening, but in retrospect he was looking out for the best interests of Hope.

First, I had to sign all sorts of legal papers, since it was going to be a single-parent adoption, saying that I would take over if anything happened to Sal. There's nothing there that I could argue otherwise. However, no one else goes through those processes. If you're legally married you don't have to. Nongay couples do not do this. It's a very rare situation.

Sal and Wayne were soon to discover that these were not the only extra steps they would have to take. For them, the battle still lay ahead. The judge decided to make their case a precedent. This would mean that in future cases of gay or lesbian adoptions, the judge or lawyers could point to Wayne and Sal's case and say, "This is legal, it's been done before."

First, the judge required that Wayne and Sal disclose their HIV status (HIV is the virus that causes AIDS). Requiring HIV status disclosure is illegal in the State of New York, and although Wayne knew this, he and Sal decided to go ahead and give this information. "Since I knew the answers," says Wayne, "we just had our doctor release our information because it was meaningless to us at this point. Politically speaking, it was totally uncalled for. But we were willing to do that."

Second, the judge appointed a *guardian ad litem*, a court-appointed guardian who must always keep the best interests of the child in mind. Much to Wayne's chagrin, the judge picked a man who was known for his conservative views. Wayne and Sal became very nervous as the possibility of losing Hope became all too real.

What was supposed to take three weeks took more than six months. The guardian never called to conduct his interviews, and it was only after Wayne and Sal complained to their attorneys that he contacted them. The guardian made his personal views well know and even berated the adoption agency for advocating placement in a gay home. When it came time for the guardian to actually visit 2-year-old Hope, Wayne says:

> For whatever reason, Hope was this little angel. She parked herself down right next to him and snuggled. He started asking her questions like "Who's this man?" pointing to Sal. "That's Daddy Sal," [Hope answered]. "Then who's this man?" [he said], pointing to me. "That's Daddy Wayne," [answered Hope].
>
> He says, "No, you can't have two daddies," and then goes into this discussion with us, with Hope in the room, about how he would not ordinarily approve this—that it is against his better judgment. However, he could see that number one, she's not wanting for anything. Number two, she is thriving. He could come up with no valid reason although he would like to disrupt the adoption.
>
> That was it. He left, and we waited and waited. He never wrote up his written report as he was required. The judge in the case almost had to subpoena him to appear at the finalization. He gave his report orally and would not put it in writing. The judge apologized for what we went through but explained that now, no one could question the adoption and, for all intents and purposes, Hope would have two daddies. Not legally, but emotionally, financially, and psychologically.

Diane also had to take a few extra steps when she petitioned to adopt her son after Patty's death. Luckily, the two women had planned ahead, and Diane at least had legal custody of Tony. But now she had to show the social workers and the *guardian ad litem* appointed to the case that she had, in fact, been another mother for Tony since he was born. Patty's brother and mother also had to tell the judge that they supported

Diane's effort. If they had not thought that Diane would be a good mother and shared this with the court, then Diane's battle would have only just begun.

As more and more alternative families begin to emerge, and as more lesbians and gay men are willing to confront the legal system, laws and attitudes will change. Research, public education, and well-adjusted kids will combine to prove that gay and lesbian families meet all the requirements of a family. . . . The law just has to catch up.

LEGAL ADVOCACY

In the 1970s and 1980s, several legal and advocacy groups came on the scene to offer services to gay and lesbian parents at little or no cost. Through national fund-raising efforts and support from individuals, these groups were able to grow and have a profound effect on the present and future of lesbian and gay parents everywhere.

One of the largest of these organizations is The Lambda Legal Defense and Education Fund (Lambda). Founded in 1973 and based in New York City, this nationally focused organization maintains offices in the Midwest and on the West Coast. The group relies on staff attorneys and volunteer attorneys to argue a variety of cases across the country. Lambda also consults with local law firms to make use of their local knowledge and resources. In addition to working on cases relating to lesbian or gay parents, Lambda assists clients who have faced discrimination based on sexual orientation in the workplace, in public accommodations such as restaurants or hotels, and or as a result of AIDS or HIV. They have handled a number of high-profile cases relating to the U.S. military's policies toward homosexuals. The organization's efforts on behalf of lesbian and gay parents has resonated in many cases, ensuring an improved climate for lesbian and gay parenting. As individuals become more and more willing to engage in such a public fight, the rights of two people of the same sex to adopt the same child will perhaps, one day, become available to men and women, gay or straight, in every city.

Until Lambda created its Family Rights Project in 1989, its main focus was not on parents' rights.[7] Realizing the need for a concerted effort to help lesbian mothers retain their rights as parents, a woman named Donna Hitchens founded the Lesbian Rights Project. This became the first organization to focus on lesbian and gay parenting issues from a legal perspective. It grew so quickly that in 1989 it was renamed the National Center for Lesbian Rights and maintains offices in San Francisco, California.[8]

Gay and lesbian parents and activists agree that whether the battle is in the courts, at school, or in the home, the best defense is a mixture of education, confronting unjust laws, and being out of the closet. Scientific studies showing no ill effects of gay parenting, the increasing number of gay and lesbian parents, and the success of the lesbian and gay rights movement have all contributed to improving the status of alternative families. The battles will rage on, but in the meantime, parents such as Julie, Lynette, Diane, Wayne, and Sal will concentrate on raising their children in the best way they know.

6
CREATING A CULTURE

Parenting can be a stressful job. Kids need a lot of attention, and parents need other parents with whom to connect and share resources. For many parents, meeting people with similar interests happens in church or synagogue, on school committees, or while their kids are playing softball. But, as welcoming as these situations seem, they are not always options for gay and lesbian parents. Because these parents may encounter homophobia, or because they are not "out," they may feel the need to hide important parts of their lives.

Where then, can they go for support and companionship which is so necessary for leading a healthy and fulfilled life?

Fifteen years ago the answer would have been that they don't have anywhere to go and that they must cope the best they can. At that time, most lesbian or gay parents did not disclose their sexual orientation. They were forced to live in an air of secrecy. A few parents and families might have discovered each other and chose to socialize. But it was clear that the traditional avenues for help and support were either not available or were too uncomfortable. This is still true today for many gay and lesbian parents living in small towns or rural areas.

Surprisingly enough, the AIDS epidemic has had a great impact on the networking of lesbian and gay parents. As community organizations developed to deal with the disease, they eventually became general meeting places for gays and lesbians. Many even began offering other social services, such as parenting and support groups. From these community groups sprang countless organizations, large and small, that now reach across America.

Often, from one organization many others have sprouted. Lesbian and gay men began identifying new needs to be met for those with children. Sometimes, informal get-togethers blossomed into full-fledged organizations or combined resources with existing gay and lesbian service groups.

The creation of Center Kids in New York City is a wonderful illustration of how a formal organization grew from an innocent informal gathering of parents who wanted to meet other gay and lesbian parents. Wayne and Sal were two of the founders of Center Kids, which is now part of the larger Gay and Lesbian Community Services Center in New York. Wayne remembers when the basic idea of lesbian and gay parents coming together dawned on him. He and Sal had been receiving phone calls from other lesbians and gay men, who wanted to know about the adoption process and how Wayne and Sal were able to get through the system. The idea of a support structure for these potential parents was mentioned.

In the summer of 1988, we decided to throw a picnic in Central Park. We invited the people whose phone numbers and addresses we had saved. We thought maybe five or six families would show up. We were surprised when fifty-five people came with fourteen children.

Almost all of them were adopted families except for one lesbian couple who was pregnant (in fact, she gave birth two weeks later). They had become pregnant through alternative insemination. Obviously, we saw a need for all of us to get together again. We did another picnic outdoors and we did an indoor gathering, and a core group of parents rose to the surface to become the leadership of this new group.

Then in February 1989, we became affiliated as the Family Project of the Lesbian and Gay Community Services Center of New York. [The long title was shortened to Center Kids, which has become the moniker for the organization.]

Center Kids was set up with a singular premise: We wanted a place for our kids to grow up knowing that they're not alone. At first everything was organized around our kids and was recreational. The purpose was for the kids to see each other, to see that oh, look, there's a family just like mine. It was before *Heather Had Two Mommies* and *Daddy's Roommate* [two books written for young children describing families with gay or lesbian parents]. It was before any visible notion of this. At least in the New York area.

Although we started off with mostly adopted families, we were very quickly joined by lesbians who were having kids through alternative insemination and a few parents who had had their kids through heterosexual marriages.

Today, Center Kids is much more than simply a place for lesbian and gay parents to get together with their children. The organization offers forums and discussion groups around issues that concern gay and lesbian parents and provides information for those who wish to become parents. All of this is scheduled around social activities designed for the kids to have fun but to also to see that they are not alone. The group has sparked interest, and other smaller groups have been formed within the outlying areas of New York City.

Just a few of the Center Kids support groups now offered include: Older Kids Rap Group, Considering Adoption, Planning Biological Parenthood, and Single Parents. There is even a group for lesbians living on the Upper West Side of New York City. There is also a Center Kids resource list containing more than twenty pages of listings of adoption agencies around the country, sperm banks, and alternative insemination facilities, attorneys and legal services, books and bookstores that might be of interest to kids and their parents, other organizations catering to lesbian and gay parents and/or their children, and other miscellaneous information.

A nationwide organization similar in nature to Center Kids has been growing consistently since 1979, when three gay fathers met at the first National March on Washington for Lesbian and Gay Rights. A year later they initiated a conference in New York under the group name The Gay Father's Coalition. Seven years later lesbian mothers joined the group, and it was renamed Gay and Lesbian Parents Coalition International (GLPCI).

GLPCI sees itself linking a wide network of local gay and lesbian parent support groups around the globe. The group has chapters in the United States, Canada, Norway, and the United Kingdom. The founders saw the need to "help [ourselves] and others in similar situations to draw upon the rich experiences . . . of [our] lives. We do this by forming supportive groups that help in building positive self-images, by networking with other gay and lesbian parents, and by educating professionals, the media, and the general public to our special strengths and unique concerns."[1]

The group's annual convention has grown considerably in recent years and attracts hundreds of families. Lynette and Julie take their three kids to the convention every year. Julie says, "I think they appreciate their participation in GLPCI and being around other kids who have two moms or two dads or whatever. With GLPCI the kids are able to meet other kids like them who have gay parents. It gives them a safe place to go, even if only just once a year. I think they've appreciated that more and more as the years go by." During the few precious days of this event, lesbian and gay families meet to discuss issues of concern and to remind their children that families like theirs can be found around the world, in small towns and big cities.

John got involved in GLPCI when he was in Chicago. He stumbled upon a local group where he met men like himself, who had come out of the closet while in heterosexual marriages and who were dealing with many emotional and logistical issues.

> It was probably this group that gave me the support that helped me do what I needed and what I wanted to do. At the time I was separated, almost every guy in this group was within three or four years of my age. Most of them were going through a separation—it was just amazing. I felt so good that I wasn't the only one. Plus, my story was so wonderful in comparison to what the rest of these guys were going through. Their wives felt very used, abused, hurt. Some went screaming through the neighborhood shouting the news to everyone and did them [the men] in financially. I didn't have any of that to deal with, so I felt very lucky. It also made me think that I was doing the right thing.

The support of other people in similar situations can be enormously helpful and uplifting. It is the backbone of organizations such as GLPCI. GLPCI's member chapters are smaller local groups that provide emotional support to lesbian mothers and gay fathers, whether they are just coming out or have been "out" lesbian or gay parents for years.

When John went back to Indianapolis from Chicago, he discovered a GLPCI chapter there. In the beginning, he found it to be a comfortable, supportive social group. But as he met more people, he discovered more meaningful aspects.

> I met people who were a lot like me, so there were people I wanted for friends because we had a lot in common. I felt this support and friendship with people who had experienced life much the same as me. Within the gay community there are certainly different factions. Gay men who have

been through a marriage and have kids aren't always the most welcome.

John became the local director of the group when it had about thirty members. He describes it as "a progression of things. I ended up going to a national conference that GLPCI put on in Atlanta in 1987. I just wanted to know what was going on with everybody else. There I met some of the most wonderful people and absolutely fell in love with them. I saw all the energy that was there and the things people were doing. I signed on to help GLPCI do some things and brought all this energy back to this local group." In 1993, John became the national president of GLPCI, and he is still involved today.

As parents began bringing their children to GLPCI events, a new group was formed. This time it was the kids themselves who decided that they wanted their own organization, apart from the adults. They formed a separate group called COLAGE, or Children of Lesbians and Gays Everywhere. COLAGE maintains its own office, produces its own mini-conference concurrent with the adults', and publishes a newsletter by kids of gays and lesbians for kids of gays and lesbians, which is sent to members around the world. Operated by the youth, COLAGE has defined its mission as follows:

> To foster the growth of daughters and sons of lesbian and gay parents by providing education, support and community on local and international levels, to advocate for our rights and those of our families and to promote acceptance and awareness in society that love makes a family.

PARENT GROUPS

Formal organizations for gay and lesbian parenting are available in towns and cities in most states. There are still many lesbian or gay parents, however, who are either not aware of their existence or who choose not to participate. Still, the need to be with other "like-minded" people remains a powerful motivator for some of these parents who form their own more casual groups.

These casual mommy and daddy groups come in all sizes and in all configurations. Usually a parent or a small group of parents decides to bring the families together, and the focus is often on the children. Joyce decided she wanted to get together with other lesbian mothers and invited a few women she knew to come with their children for a very informal afternoon.

She knew several other lesbian parents who had no biological or extended family to provide any type of support. She realized how important a support system was for her and Michael.

> I wanted Michael to have other kids that came from the same type of family. I want him to know that being in a heterosexual family isn't the only way that there is [to live]. My friend and I said, "Okay, let's start this mothers group." We originally called all the women we knew who had A.I. [alternative insemination] babies and told them what we were doing.
>
> We held the first gathering two years ago, here in my home, and we had all the kids with us. It was so cute. The kids were little babies—the youngest was six weeks old. Now, it's insane because everybody's walking and running and talking and screaming, and our mothers' group has grown to about twenty or thirty.
>
> When we started no one was single, but now I'm not with my original partner, and two other women are not with their original partners. But we all still come together. We've also expanded, and now have one couple who adopted a baby from South America. I also invited another friend who has a child Michael's age even though he wasn't an A.I. baby.

We don't do anything serious. It's just very social. The kids play, and we hang out. I wanted this group for me because I felt it was hard for me to go to events and do things and connect with people because I had a child. People aren't always supportive of that. As mothers, we wanted to know each other. We wanted to have a network of people that we knew and that we could get to know and that our kids could know.

HEALTH CENTERS

Centers specializing in lesbian or women's health have been on the rise, and those providing alternative insemination services now serve many lesbians. A San Francisco clinic, Pacific Reproductive Services, says more than one hundred lesbians use the sperm bank each month.[2] Medical clinics that cater to gay or lesbian clients can be found in many major cities including the Howard Brown Health Center (formerly the Howard Brown Memorial Clinic) in Chicago, Whitman-Walker Clinic in Washington, D.C., and the Lyon-Martin Women's Health Services in San Francisco (named for lesbian activists Del Lyon and Phyllis Martin).

The Lyon-Martin Women's Health Services, a community clinic, focuses largely on lesbians and bisexual women. In addition to medical services, Lyon-Martin offers services for lesbian and gay families. It sponsors the Lyon-Martin Lesbian/Gay Parenting Services (LGPS) for prospective parents, as well as those families that already have children. LGPS offers information and referrals, forums, support groups, workshops and special events.[3]

Medical clinics, national groups, volunteers . . . in special ways these types of organizations form a strong chain for lesbian and gay parents. Through forums on adoption, insemination services, or merely picnics in the park, these programs provide essential communication and emotional links for parents and kids who might easily feel isolated or not represented in larger society. As John discovered when he first attended a GLPCI support group, the chance to meet and socialize with other lesbian and gay parents, to find that some of their lives mirror your own, provides a kind of emotional and practical support that helps dissolve feelings of isolation.

This national and natural connection to other people has helped make a culture for gay and lesbian families by gay and lesbian families, replete with sensitive and interested women and men across the country. In large cities and small, the network is growing. Informal gatherings, such as Joyce's mommy group, are just as powerful and vital as larger organizations such as Center Kids or GLPCI. Whatever its format or specific mission, each group affirms the rewards and pains of child-rearing as well as the special challenges of being a lesbian or gay parent in America. Each group is there to help, to teach, and to lend a hand when needed.

It is important to credit the difficult work that has been accomplished by such groups in educating the public and promoting positive images—rather than the myths and stereotypes that have for so long plagued lesbians and gay men. But their true service has been to create a national family offering love and support.

How do you define "family"?

As any lesbian or gay parent will tell you, love makes a family!

SOURCE NOTES

Introduction

1. Quoted from Hillary Rodham Clinton's speech to the graduating class of The George Washington University on Sunday, May 8, 1994.

Chapter One

1. J. Seligmann, "Variations on a Theme," *Newsweek* Special Edition: "The 21st Century Family," Winter/Spring 1990, pp. 38–46.

2. *Statistical Abstract of the U.S.*, 1993, 113th edition, pp. 5–6.

3. Seligmann, pp. 38–46.

4. Charlotte Patterson, "Children of Lesbian and Gay Parents," *Child Development*, 1992, vol. 63, pp. 1025–1042.

5. Kinsey, *Sexual Behavior in the Human Female* (W.B. Saunders, 1963).

6. Patterson.

7. American Bar Association study, 1988.

8. Paul Varnell, "News Digest: Around the Nation," *Windy City Times*, July 14, 1994, p. 10.

9. *Partners* national survey, 1990.

10. Charlotte Patterson, "Lesbian and Gay Couples Considering Parenthood: An Agenda for Research, Service, and Advocacy," *Journal of Gay & Lesbian Social Services*, 1993.

11. Patterson, "Children of Lesbian and Gay Parents," pp. 1025–1042.

12. Susan Chira, "Gay and Lesbian Parents Grow More Visible," *New York Times*, September 30, 1993, p. A1..

13. Patterson, "Children of Lesbian and Gay Parents," pp. 1025–1042.

14. Daniel Goleman, "Studies Find No Disadvantages in Growing Up in a Gay Home," *New York Times*, December 2, 1992.

15. Mucklow, *Psych Reports* 44:880, 1979; Green, *American Journal of Psychiatry,* 135:692, 1978; Hoeffer, *American Journal of Orthopsychiatry,* 51:536, 1981; Kirkpatrick, *Journal of Homosexuality,* 14:20, 1987; Hall, *Social Work,* 23:380, 1978; Susoff, *UCLA Law Review,* 32:4, 1985.

Chapter Two

1. Wendell Ricketts and Roberta Achtenberg, "Adoption and Foster Parenting for Lesbians and Gay Men: Creating New Traditions in Family," in Frederick W. Bozett, ed., *Homosexuality and Family Relations* (New York: Hawotth Press, 1990).

2. A lesbian couple, Sharon Kowalski and Karen Thompson, had their lives turned upside down when Sharon had an accident and subsequently fell into a vegetative state. Karen was thrown into a battle for caretakership with Sharon's parents. Because Sharon and Karen had not previously come out as a lesbian couple, Karen found herself with no rights allowing her to be at Sharon's bedside. She was also not allowed to make medical decisions for her. Sharon's family fought in court to keep Karen from winning any caretaker's rights. The case ended several years later, when the courts granted Karen full rights and allowed her to care for Sharon.

Chapter Three

1. *Heather Has Two Mommies* (Boston: Alyson Publications, 1991) is a children's book written by Leslea Newman that

details life with two moms from their young daughter's point of view. It illustrates that lesbian households may be different, but not wrong.

Chapter Five

1. Judy Grahn, *Another Mother Tongue: Gay Words, Gay Worlds* (Boston: Beacon Press, 1984), p. 303.

2. Leigh W. Rutledge, *The Gay Decades* (New York: Plume Books, 1992), p. 208.

3. Rutledge, p. 312.

4. *Statistical Abstract of the United States*, U.S. Department of Commerce, pp. 5–6.

5. Jane Gross, "After a Ruling Hawaii Weights Gay Marriages," *New York Times*, April 25, 1994, p. A1.

6. Jean Seligmann, "Variations on a Theme," *Newsweek*, Special Edition: "The 21st Century Family," Winter/Spring, 1990, p.38.

7. Laura Benkov, *Reinventing the Family* (New York: Crown Publishers, 1994), p. 35.

8. Benkov, p. 35.

Chapter Six

1. Gay and Lesbian Parents Coalition International pamphlet.

2. William H. Henry, "Gay Parents: Under Fire and on the Rise," *Time*, September 20, 1993.

3. Charlotte Patterson, "Lesbian and Gay Couples Considering Parenthood: An Agenda for Research, Service, and Advocacy," *Journal of Gay and Lesbian Social Services*, 1993.

RESOURCES

GAY AND LESBIAN PARENTS COALITION INTERNATIONAL

The Gay and Lesbian Parents Coalition International (GLPCI) is an advocacy and support organization of lesbian mothers, gay fathers, bisexual parents, their partners and children. They have more than eighty-five chapters in eight countries. GLPCI can provide information and referrals on custody issues, adoption, surrogacy, A.I., and the rights of coparents.

For additional information or to receive their quarterly newsletter, send your name and postal address to GLPCI at the address listed below, or e-mail them at GLPCINat@ix.net-com.com.

Their mailing list is kept confidential and is never given to other organizations or groups.

They also have an organization for children of gay or lesbian parents, Children of Lesbians and Gays Everywhere (COLAGE), that can be reached at the conventional or e-mail addresses listed under *Resources for Children*. COLAGE offers a quarterly newsletter and support groups facilitated by trained professionals for children age twelve and above.

GLPCI Directory of Resources

Gay and Lesbian Parents Coalition International (GLPCI)
P.O. Box 50360

Washington, DC 20091
Phone: (202) 583-8029
Fax: (201) 783-6204
E-mail: FamValues@aol.com or GLCPINat@ix.netcom.com

Executive Director
Tim Fisher
538 Park Street
Montclair, NJ 07043
Phone/Fax: (201) 783-6204

COLAGE Representative
Stefan Lynch
423 Capp Street
San Francisco, CA 94110
(415) 206-1930

In Canada
GLPCI
c/o Gay Fathers of Toronto
Box 187
Station F
Toronto, Ontario, M4Y 2L5
CANADA

GLPCI Member Chapters/Affiliated Organizations
(Chapters are listed alphabetically by country, province/state, and city.)

CANADA
MANITOBA
Gay Fathers of Winnipeg
P.O. Box 2221
Winnipeg, Manitoba R3C 3R5
Phone: Glenn Fewster, (204) 943-1556

ONTARIO
Gay Fathers of Toronto
Box 187
Station F
Toronto, Ontario M4Y 2L5
Phone: Brian Moore, (800) 975-1680

UNITED KINGDOM

My Mums' Group
c/o Babs Greenwood
Flat 5
1 South View
Teignmouth, Devon TQ14 8BJ
England
Phone: + 44 626 778926

UNITED STATES

Alabama

Gay and Lesbian Parents Coalition International—
    Gulf Coast Chapter
c/o Priscilla Vaughan
P.O. Box 1990
Semmes, AL 36575-1990
Phone: (205) 476-1309

Arizona

Gay and Lesbian Parent Support Network
Box 66823
Phoenix, AZ 85082-6823
Phone: Debby Merritt, (602) 926-9296

Gay, Lesbian and Bisexual Parents Network
c/o Wingspan
422 North 4th Avenue
Tucson, AZ 85705

Phone: Craig Oakes, (602) 318-9348 or Lisa McAllister, (602) 624-7376

California
Bakersfield Parents Group
2002 19th Street
Bakersfield, CA 93301
Phone: Mike or Mary Bensusen, (805) 322-9772

The Kid's Klub
c/o Elizabeth River
992 Jonell Lane
Chico, CA 95926
Phone: (916) 343-7208

Lesbian Mothers and Our Children
c/o C. Skelly
3100 Buckingham Road
Glendale, CA 91206

Gay Fathers of Long Beach
2017 East 4th Street
Long Beach, CA 90804
Phone: Jerry, (310) 423-5313 or Doug, (714) 744-2957

Lesbian Mothers of Long Beach
c/o CORE
1401 East 4th Street, Suite C
Long Beach, CA 90802
Phone: (310) 495-9206

Gay Fathers of Los Angeles
7985 Santa Monica Boulevard, Suite 109-346
West Hollywood, CA 90046
Phone: Lee Dubin, (213) 654-0307

Lesbian Mothers and Our Children
c/o GLCSC-COEP
1625 North Hudson Ave.

Los Angeles, CA 90028
Phone: Millie Ben-David, (213) 654-4722; or
    GLCSC, (213) 993-7432

Rainbow Families of Southern California
4565 Anne Sladon Street
Oceanside, CA 92057
Phone: Richele Daciolas-Semon, (619) 439-8928

Lesbian/Gay Parents Association
6705 California Street, #1
San Francisco, CA 94121
(415) 387-9886

Baylands Family Circle
Billy DeFrank Community Center
175 Stockton Avenue
San Jose, CA 95126
Phone: Hotline, (408) 251-8766

Santa Cruz Lesbian Mothers Group
c/o Ellen Farmer
P.O. Box 5296
Santa Cruz, CA 95063

Connecticut
Connecticut Lesbian Moms' Support & Play Group
W. Hartford, CT

Connecticut and Rhode Island Gay and Lesbian Parents
    Support Group
Hartford, CT—contact GLPCI

District of Columbia
Gay Fathers Coalition of Washington, DC
P.O. Box 19891
Washington, D.C. 20036
Phone: Ron Lewis, (301) 990-9522

Florida
Lesbigay Parents and Our Kids
c/o Beth St. Rose
830 NE 71st
Miami FL 33138
Phone: (305) 758-0392

Gay and Lesbian Parents Coalition International—
    Central Florida Chapter
Box 561504
Orlando, FL 32856
Phone: (407) 420-2191

Georgia
Gay Fathers of Atlanta
10 Hillside Drive
Carterville, GA 30120
Phone: Lee Bright, (404) 386-6161

Lesbian and Gay Parents Coalition
P.O. Box 2107
Decatur, GA 30031

Hawaii
We Are Family
1995 Tenth Avenue
Honolulu, HI 96816
Phone: (808) 735-3911

Illinois
Family Circle
4156 West School Street
Second Floor
Chicago, IL 60641
Phone: Mary Silas and Helen Bielski,
    (312) 283-6619

LParents with Pride
c/o Rebecca Thompson
1511 Trainer Road
Rockford, IL 61108
Phone: Barb Blecker, (815) 227-1831

Indiana
Gay and Lesbian Parents Coalition of Indianapolis
P.O. Box 831
Indianapolis, IN 46206
Phone: Terry Snoeberger, (317) 926-9741, or
    Vickie Harris, (317) 353-6636

Kansas
Wichita Lesbian Mothers Group
c/o Visions and Dreams
3143 West Maple
Wichita, KS 67213
Phone: Renee Tucker-Fletcher, (316) 942-6333

Maine
Gay, Lesbian, Bisexual Parents of Maine
P.O. Box 13
Augusta, ME 04332-0013
Phone: Frank Brooks, (207) 772-4741

Maryland
Families with Pride
c/o Susan Wirth
423 Winston Avenue
Baltimore, MD 21212
Phone: (410) 435-7261

Gay Fathers Coalition of Baltimore
P.O. Box 1286
Hunt Valley, MD 21030
Phone: John E. Crockett II, (410) 666-5762

Gay and Lesbian Parents Coalition—Metro Washington
c/o Jim Fagelson
14908 Piney Grove Court
Gaithersburg, MD 20878
Phone: (301) 762-4828

Massachusetts
Gay Fathers of Greater Boston
Box 1373
Boston, MA 02205
Phone: Alan Gray, (617) 273-1740,
    GFGB Outreach, (617) 742-7897

Lesbian/Gay Family and Parenting Services Program
Fenway Community Health Center
7 Haviland Street
Boston, MA 02115
Phone: Jenifer Firestone
(617) 267-0900, ext. 282

Lesbian Mothers of Metro-Boston
c/o Barr/Fraas
131-B Laurel Street
Malden, MA 02148
Phone: (617) 397-8408

Michigan
Gay and Lesbian Parents Association
Detroit, MI—contact GLPCI

Gay and Lesbian Parents Coalition of Michigan [Detroit]
P.O. Box 472
Farmington, MI 48332
Phone: (313) 291-0937

Minnesota
Minnesota Families
P.O. Box 11386
St. Paul, MN 55111

Phone: Denny Siemers, (612) 897-1281

Mississippi
Jackson Parents Group
c/o John W. Morgan III
1677 Wilhurst Street
Jackson, MS 39211
Phone: (601) 362-6854

Missouri
Parents of Greater Kansas City
8510 Stark
Raytown, MO 64138
Phone: Dawn and Dona, (816) 353-3492

Free to Be Families
c/o Elizabeth Nolan
24 Ladel Court
St. Louis, MO 63132
Phone: (314) 777-7313

New Jersey
Lambda Families of New Jersey [Morristown]
c/o Aimee Gelnaw
35 Lexington Avenue
Montclair, NJ 07042
Phone: (201) 744-4649

Central Jersey Families
c/o Central Jersey Alliance
P.O. Box 909
Plainfield, NJ 07601-0909
Phone: Julie and Tricia, (908) 756-4955, or
    Donna, (908) 752-9265

New Mexico
DλDS of New Mexico
Box 1254
Santa Fe, NM 87504-1254

New York

Lambda Family Circle
c/o Cindy Crumrine and Ann Loughman
101 South Pine Avenue
Albany, NY 12208
(518) 482-3268

Gay Fathers Coalition of Buffalo
Box 404
Westside Station
Buffalo, NY 14213

Gay Fathers of Brooklyn
c/o William P. Ciardiello
17A Fuller Court
Staten Island, NY 10306-6134
Phone: (718) 979-5283

Lesbians Choosing Children
c/o Lawton/Warren
11A Brookside Avenue
Chatham, NY 12037
Phone: (518) 766-9697

Center Kids
c/o The Lesbian and Gay Community Services Center
208 West 13th Street
New York, NY 10011
Phone: (212) 620-7310, or Wayne Steinman, (718) 987-6747

Gay Fathers I of New York
c/o Robert Boxer
194 Riverside Drive
New York, NY 10025
Phone: (212) 874-7727

New York Gay & Bisexual Married Men's Group
c/o Jerry Megna
853 Weber Drive
Yardley, PA 19067
Phone: (215) 493-8197

Gay Fathers of Long Island
P.O. Box 2483
Patchogue, NY 11772
Phone: Brian, (516) 282-9478

Gay Fathers of Westchester
Box 686
Croton Falls, NY 10519
Phone: Tom, (914) 276-2614

Ohio
Gay & Lesbian Parents Group of Central
    Ohio [Columbus]
P.O. Box 16235
Columbus, OH 43216
Phone: Ross Schifano and Tim Dick, (614) 764-2556

Gay and Lesbian Parents—Northeast Ohio
3804 Morley Drive
Kent, OH 44240
Phone: (216) 677-9856

H.U.G.S. East
c/o Karen Harmnack
8497 Johnnycake Ridge
Mentor, OH 44060
Phone: (216) 255-2156, or Terrie Doboze, (216) 261-3206

Oregon
Love Makes a Family, Inc.
P.O. Box 11694
Portland, OR 97211
Phone: Bonnie Tinker, (503) 228-3892

Pennsylvania
Philadelphia Area Lesbian Mothers Group
7419 Elizabeth Road
Melrose Park, PA 19126
Phone: (215) 635-6291

Philadelphia Family Pride
P.O. Box 4995
Philadelphia, PA 19119
Phone: Tish Fabens or Marla Gold, (215) 843-1596

Gay Fathers of Pittsburgh
c/o Ben Skinker
6743 Stanton Avenue
Pittsburgh, PA 15206-1767
Phone: (412) 361-3557

Lesbians Are Parents
P.O. Box 19202
Pittsburgh, PA 15213
Phone: Janice Anderson, (412) 371-2383

Puerto Rico
Puerto Rico Gay and Lesbian Parents Group
Box 116
1505 Calle Loiza
Santurce, PR 00911
Phone: Boris Oxman, (809) 726-2888

Tennessee
Nashville Parents Group
P.O. Box 60933
Nashville, TN 37206

Texas
Dallas GLPCI/Parents Group
P.O. Box 154031
Irving, TX 75015-4031
Phone: John R. Selig, (214) 490-3821

Gay Fathers/Fathers First of Houston
P.O. Box 981053
Houston, TX 77098

Houston Gay and Lesbian Parents
P.O. Box 35709-262

Houston, TX 77235-5709
Phone: Ellen, (713) 980-7995

Tarrant County Gay/Lesbian Parents Group
Box 48382
Watauga, TX 76148-0382
Phone: (817) 656-8056

Vermont
Vermont Lesbian and Gay Parents
c/o Out in the Mountains
P.O. Box 177
Burlington, VT 05401
Phone: Deborah Lashman and
     Jane Van Buren, (802) 660-2713

Gay Fathers Connection
Box 5506
Essex Junction, VT 05453-5506

Virginia
We Are Families [DC/No. VA/MD]
P.O. Box 935
Great Falls, VA 22066
Phone: (800) 225-0256, ext. 45073

Washington
Out on a L.I.M.B. (Lesbians in
     Maternity and Beyond)
c/o Pat Justis and Terry Murphy
6306 Snug Harbor Court NE
Olympia, WA 98506
(206) 459-5221

Gay Fathers Association of Seattle
P.O. Box 654
Edmonds, WA 98020
Phone: Larry Bailey, (206) 774-7528

South Puget Sound Lesbian and Gay Parents Support Group
c/o TLC Post Office Box 947
Tacoma. WA 98401
(206) 472-0422, or Carol (206) 472-4446

NATIONWIDE
Adoption Resource Exchange for Single Parents
P.O. Box 5782
Springfield, VA 22150
Phone: (703) 866-5577

Future Gay Fathers of America
P.O. Box 43206
Montclair, NJ 07043
Phone: Wayne Steinman (adoption),
    (718) 987-6747, or Tim Fisher (surrogacy),
    (201) 783-6204 (phone and fax)

Support for Straight Spouses
Amity Pierce Buxton (author of *The Other
    Side of the Closet*)
8215 Terrace Drive
El Cerrito, CA 94530
Phone: (510) 525-0200

Resources for Children
Children of Lesbians and Gays Everywhere (COLAGE)
2300 Market Street
Box 165
San Francisco, CA 94114
E-mail: KidsOfGays@aol.com

In Canada
COLAGE
Box 187
Station F
Toronto, Ontario M4Y 2L5
CANADA

LOCAL SUPPORT GROUPS

California
Teens Relating Unique Situations Together (TRUST)
106 Thorn Street
San Diego, CA 92103

COLAGE Coffee Klatch (adult children)
2300 Market Street, #165
San Francisco, CA 94114

COLAGE/East Bay
582 Arguleeo Boulevard
San Francisco, CA 94118

COLAGE/San Francisco
3361-A 21st Street
San Francisco, CA 94110

Gaybies
c/o First Unitarian Church
160 North 3rd Street
San Jose, CA 95112

Just For Us— Los Angeles
7985 Santa Monica Boulevard, Suite 109-346
West Hollywood, CA 90046

District of Columbia
COLAGE/Gay Fathers Coalition
Box 19891
Washington, DC 20036

Indiana
Our Parents Aren't Straight (OPAS)
P.O. Box 831
Indianapolis, IN 46206

Massachusetts
Just For Us—Boston
11 Lovell Street #2
Somerville, MA 02144

Michigan
Just For Us—Michigan
c/o GLPCM
P.O. Box 1084
Troy, MI 48099

Minnesota
COLAGE/The Bridge
2300 Emerson Avenue South
Minneapolis, MN 55405

New York
Older Kids Rap Group
141 Columbia Heights, #3C
New York, NY 10011

Second Generation (lesbian and gay kids of lesbian
    and gay parents)
57 Second Avenue, Apt. 51
New York, NY 10003

Texas
Teens Relating Unique Situations Together (TRUST)
3141 Hood, Suite 616
Dallas, TX 75219

Just for Us—Houston
4122 Sarong Drive
Houston, TX 77025-4616

Washington
Teens of Gays Everywhere
8824 Sherman Valley Road
Olympia, WA 98512

OTHER RESOURCES
Lavender Families (formerly Lesbian Mothers' National
    Defense Fund)
P.O Box 21567

Seattle, WA 98111
Phone: (206) 325-2643

Momazons
P.O. Box 02069
Columbus, OH 43202
Phone: (614) 267-0193

Custody Action for Lesbian Mothers (CALM)
P.O. Box 281
Narberth, PA 19072

Chain of Life (feminist adoption newsletter)
P.O. Box 8081
Berkeley, CA 94707

The Family Next Door (lesbian and gay parenting
   newsletter)
Next Door Publishing, Ltd.
Box 212580
Oakland, CA 94620

INTERNET RESOURCES

List Servers
To get a sorted directory of list servers relating to lesbian, gay,
   and bisexual issues send mail to:

listserv@umdd.umd.edu

The text of the e-mail should be:

get lesbigay lists wmst-l

QUEER-PARENTS is a discussion list for lesbian, gay, or bi
moms, dads, co-moms, co-dads, and mommy and daddy
wanna-bes. It is intended to provide a supportive virtual space
for the parenting concerns of lesbian and gay men and queer-
identified bis. Networking is encouraged! The list is unmoderated.

Subscriptions and posting:

To SUBSCRIBE to QUEER-PARENTS send mail to:

majordomo@vector.casti.com
subject: <none>
Text:

subscribe QUEER-PARENTS

To POST:

Send mail to: QUEER-PARENTS@vector.casti.com

Your message will be distributed to the entire list. Do not send subscription-type requests to this address!

To UNSUBSCRIBE from QUEER-PARENTS, or to change your e-address, send mail to:
majordomo@vector.casti.com
Cc:
Subject: <none>

unsubscribe QUEER-PARENTS

Majordomo is a computer program. You must send messages directly to the program to get on or off the list. For more information on commands that majordomo will honor, send the message "help" to majordomo@vector.casti.com.

GAYDADS is a discussion list for gay/bi dads, co-dads, and daddy wanna-bes. It is intended to provide a supportive virtual space for the parenting concerns of gay men. The list is unmoderated. GAYDADS is a companion to the MOMS list, started in 1993 by Dorsie Hathaway and Darci Chapman. This list is for men. For mixed discussion, subscribe to the QUEER-PARENTS list using the same address.

Other questions should be addressed to:

dhathaway@pomona.claremont.edu

Subscriptions and posting:

To SUBSCRIBE to GAYDADS send mail to:

majordomo@vector.casti.com
subject: <none>
Text:

subscribe GAYDADS

To POST:

Send mail to: GAYDADS@vector.casti.com

Your message will be distributed to the entire list. Do not send subscription-type requests to this address!

To UNSUBSCRIBE from GAYDADS, or to change your e-mail address, send mail to:
majordomo@vector.casti.com
Cc:
Subject: <none>

unsubscribe GAYDADS

The *moms* mailing list is for lesbian mothers, lesbian co-moms, and lesbian mom-wannabes. This list is for women only. For mixed discussion, subscribe to the QUEER-PARENTS list. All subscription requests will be approved manually by the list owner. While this list is unmoderated, it is also a private list, meaning that only subscribers will be allowed to post to the list and make other moms list specific queries of majordomo. The moms list is a companion to the GAYDADS list.

To post to the moms list use:
moms@qiclab.scn.rain.com

All moms REQUESTS should be sent to:
majordomo@qiclab.scn.rain.com

To SUBSCRIBE
Send in the BODY of your e-mail:

>subscribe moms Your Name <your e-mail address>

For example:

>subscribe moms Darci Chapman <dlc@gasco.com>

Leaving your name out will only delay the subscribe process. Don't leave it out.

To UNSUBSCRIBE
Send in the BODY of your e-mail and from the same account you subscribed from:

>unsubscribe moms

If you need to UNSUBSCRIBE from a different account than the one you originally subscribed to, use:

>unsubscribe moms <e-mail address of other account>

Other COMMANDS
If you are unsure which account you subscribed from, list members may use:

>who moms

(which will return all list members)
or use:

>which Your Name

(which will just return the line with Your Name on it)

For a complete list of commands send:

>help

If all else FAILS
IF you have tried all the above (especially "help") and your problem still remains unresolved, you may reach the human being responsible for the moms list by sending e-mail to moms-approval@qiclab.scn.rain.com

Domestic Partners is a mailing list dealing with all issues regarding domestic partnerships, including legal issues and strategies for obtaining benefits from employees.

Subscriptions and posting:

To SUBSCRIBE to Domestic Partners

Send subscription inquiries to:

domestic-request@tattoo.mti.sgi.com

Post to:

domestic@tattoo.mti.sgi.com

LINKS TO LESBIAN, GAY, AND BISEXUAL RESOURCES

World Wide Web
http://akebono.stanford.edu/yahoo/Society_and_Culture/Sex/
Homosexual_and_Bisexual_Resources/
http://www.cs.cmu.edu:8001/Web/People/mjw/Queer/
MainPage.html

Gopher
uclink.berkeley.edu
Choose *Other U.C. Berkeley Information Servers | Community Topics | Multicultural/Bisexual Lesbian Gay Alliance*

Usenet New Groups
These groups will give you up-to-the-minute news on all gay and lesbian issues:
clari.news.gays
clari.news.group.gays
Read about all sorts of parenting and family issues in these groups:
clari.news.family
clari.news.issues.family
clari.news.children

Additional Internet Resources
The QRD (short for Queer Resources Directory) is an electronic library with news clippings, political contact information, newsletters, essays, images, and every other kind of information resource of interest to the gay, lesbian, and bisex-

ual community. Information is stored for the use of casual network users and serious researchers alike.

Accessing QRD

The QRD FTP site is located at:
ftp.qrd.org

Log in as *anonymous* or *ftp* and at the password prompt, enter your e-mail address—make sure it has an @ sign, or you will be denied access. Then enter:
cd /pub/QRD

The QRD Gopher site is located at:
gopher.qrd.org

Select *Queer Resources*.

The QRD World Wide Web home page is located at:
http://www.qrd.org/QRD/

The QRD *Frequently Asked Questions* (FAQ) document is located in the following directories:

pub/QRD/qrdinfo/qrd-faq
    or
pub/QRD/0FREQUENTLY-ASKED-QUESTIONS

You can also get it by e-mailing any kind of message to info@qrd.org

BIBLIOGRAPHY

BOOKS ON PARENTING

Alpert, Harriet, ed. *We Are Everywhere*. Freedom, Calif.: Crossing Press, 1988.

Barret, Robert L. *Gay Fathers*. Lexington, Mass.: Lexington Books, 1990.

Benkov, Laura. *Reinventing the Family: The Emerging Story of Lesbian and Gay Parents*. New York: Crown Publishers, 1994.

Bozett, Frederick W., ed. *Gay and Lesbian Parents*. New York: Praeger, 1987.

Burke, Phyllis. *Family Values: A Lesbian Mother's Fight for Her Son*. New York: Vintage, 1994.

Buxton, Amity. *The Other Side of the Closet : The Coming-out Crisis for Straight Spouses and Families*. Rev. and expanded. New York: Wiley, 1994.

Corley, Rip. *The Final Closet: A Gay Parent's Guide for Coming Out to Their Children*. Miami: Editech Press, 1990.

Gantz, Joe. *Whose Child Cries: Children of Gay Parents Talk about Their Lives*. Rolling Hills Estates, Calif.: Jalmar Press, 1983.

Gay Fathers: Some of Their Stories, Experience, and Advice. Toronto: Gay Fathers of Toronto, 1981.

Gibson, Gifford Guy. *By Her Own Admission: A Lesbian Mother's Fight to Keep Her Son*. Garden City, N.Y.: Doubleday, 1977.

Hanscombe, Gillian E., and Jackie Forster. *Rocking the Cradle: Lesbian Mothers: A Challenge in Family Living*. Boston: Alyson, 1982.

Jenness, Aylette. *Families: A Celebration of Diversity, Commitment, and Love*. Boston: Houghton Mifflin, 1989.

Jullion, Jeanne. *Long Way Home: The Odyssey of a Lesbian Mother and Her Children*. San Francisco: Cleis Press, 1985.

Lewin, Ellen. *Lesbian Mothers: Accounts of Gender in American Culture*. Ithaca, N.Y.: Cornell University Press, 1993.

Martin, April. *The Lesbian and Gay Parenting Handbook: Creating and Raising Our Families*. New York: HarperPerennial, 1993.

McNeill, John J. *Taking a Chance on God: Liberating Theology for Gays, Lesbians, and Their Lovers, Families, and Friends*. Boston: Beacon Press, 1988.

Meyers, Diana T., Kenneth Kipnis, and Cornelius F. Murphy, Jr., eds. *Kindred Matters: Rethinking the Philosophy of the Family*. Ithaca, N.Y.: Cornell University Press, 1993.

Miller, Deborah A. *Coping When a Parent Is Gay*. New York: Rosen Pub. Group, 1993.

Pies, Cheri. *Considering Parenthood*. 2nd ed., updated. San Francisco: Spinsters/Aunt Lute, 1988.

Pollack, Sandra, and Jeanne Vaughn, eds. *Politics of the Heart: A Lesbian Parenting Anthology*. Ithaca, N.Y.: Firebrand Books, 1987.

Rafkin, Louise. *Different Mothers: Sons and Daughters of Lesbians Talk about Their Lives*. Pittsburgh: Cleis Press, 1990.

Ricketts, Wendell. *Lesbians and Gay Men As Foster Parents*. Portland, Me.: National Child Welfare Resource Center, Center for Child and Family Policy, Edmund S. Muskie Institute of Public Affairs, University of Southern Maine, 1991.

Rofes, Eric, and Students at Fayerweather Street School. *The Kids' Book about Parents*. Boston: Houghton Mifflin, 1984.

Schulenburg, Joy A. *Gay Parenting*. Garden City, N.Y.: Anchor Press/Doubleday, 1985.

Weston, Kath. *Families We Choose: Lesbians, Gays, Kinship.* New York: Columbia University Press, 1991.

FICTION ABOUT LESBIAN AND GAY PARENTING

Bergman, Susan. *Anonymity.* New York: Farrar, Straus and Giroux, 1994.

Bills, Greg. *Consider This Home.* New York: Simon and Schuster, 1994.

Ferrell, Anderson. *Home for the Day.* New York: Knopf, 1994.

BOOKS FOR CHILDREN AND YOUNG ADULTS

Leavitt, David. *The Lost Language of Cranes.* New York: Knopf, 1986.

Newman, Leslea. *Gloria Goes to Gay Pride.* Illustrated by Russell Crocker. Boston: Alyson Wonderland, 1991.

————. *Heather Has Two Mommies.*Illustrated by Diana Souza. Boston: Alyson Wonderland, 1989.

————. *Saturday Is Pattyday.* Illustrated by Annette Hegel. Norwich, Vt.: New Victoria, 1993.

Valentine, Johnny. *Two Moms, the Zark and Me.* Illustrated by Angelo Lopez. Boston: Alyson Wonderland, 1993.

Willhoite, Michael. *Daddy's Roommate.* Boston: Alyson Wonderland, 1990.

BOOKS ON LESBIAN AND GAY HISTORY AND LIBERATION

Adam, Barry D. *The Rise of a Gay and Lesbian Movement.* Boston: Twayne Publishers, 1987.

Altman, Dennis. *Homosexual : Oppression and Liberation.* New York: New York University Press, 1993.

Boswell, John. *Rediscovering Gay History: Archetypes of Gay Love in Christian History.* London: Gay Christian Movement, 1982.

Chauncey, George. *Gay New York: Gender, Urban Culture, and* the Making of the Gay Male World, 1890–1940. New York: Basic Books, 1994.

Cohen, Susan, and Daniel Cohen. *When Someone You Know Is Gay*. New York: Laurel-Leaf Books, 1992, 1989.

Collis, Rose. *Portraits to the Wall: Historic Lesbian Lives Unveiled*. New York: Cassell, 1994.

Cruikshank, Margaret. *The Gay and Lesbian Liberation Movement*. New York: Routledge, 1992.

D'Emilio, John. *Making Trouble:Essays on Gay History, Politics, and the University*. New York: Routledge, 1992.

Duberman, Martin B. *About Time: Exploring the Gay Past*. Rev. and expanded ed. New York: Meridian, 1991.

————. *Stonewall*. New York: Dutton, 1993.

————, Martha Vicinus, and George Chauncey, Jr., eds. *Hidden from History: Reclaiming the Gay and Lesbian Past*. New York: Penguin, 1989.

Faderman, Lillian. *Odd Girls and Twilight Lovers: A History of Lesbian Life in Twentieth-Century America*. New York: Penguin, 1992.

————. *Surpassing the Love of Men: Romantic Friendship and Love between Women, from the Renaissance to the Present*. New York: Morrow, 1981.

Holbrook, Sabra. *Fighting Back: The Struggle for Gay Rights*. New York: Dutton, 1987.

Jay, Karla, and Allen Young, eds. *Out of the Closets: Voices of Gay Liberation*. 2nd ed. New York : New York University Press, 1992.

Katz, Jonathan Ned. *Gay American History: Lesbians and Gay Men in the U.S.A., a Documentary History*. Rev. ed. New York: Meridian, 1992.

————. *Gay/Lesbian Almanac: A New Documentary in Which Is Contained, in Chronological Order, Evidence of the True and Fantastical History of Those Persons Now Called Lesbians and Gay Men*. New York: Harper & Row, 1983.

Marcus, Eric. *Making History: The Struggle for Gay and Lesbian*

Equal Rights, 1945–1990: An Oral History. New York: HarperCollins, 1992.

McCuen, Gary E. *Homosexuality and Gay Rights*. Hudson, Wis.: G. E. McCuen Publications, 1994.

Richards, Dell. *Lesbian Lists: A Look at Lesbian Culture, History, and Personalities*. Boston: Alyson Publications, 1990.

Rutledge, Leigh W. *The Gay Decades: From Stonewall to the Present, the People and Events That Shaped Gay Lives*. New York: Plume, 1992.

———. *The Gay Fireside Companion*. Boston: Alyson, 1989.

Thompson, Mark, ed. *Long Road to Freedom*. New York: St. Martin's Press, 1994.

Vacha, Keith. *Quiet Fire: Memoirs of Older Gay Men*. Trumansburg, N.Y. : Crossing Press, 1985.

Weeks, Jeffrey. *Against Nature: Essays on History, Sexuality and Identity*. Concord, Mass. : Paul and Co., 1991.

———. *Coming Out: Homosexual Politics in Britain from the Nineteenth Century to the Present*. New York: Quartet Books, 1977.

Weiss, Andrea, and Greta Schiller. *Before Stonewall : The Making of a Gay and Lesbian Community*. Tallahassee, Fla.: Naiad Press, 1988.

INDEX

lang, k.d., 58
Legal advocacy, 96
Legal Defense and
    Education Fund
    (Lambda), 96, 97
Legal issues, 19, 24, 26, 33,
    34, 35, 36, 37, 41, 43,
    44, 45, 53, 54, 81–82,
    88, 91, 96–97. *See also*
    Civil rights
Lesbian Rights Project, 97.
    See also National Center
    for Lesbian Rights
Lorde, Audre, 91
Lotus Development
    Corporation, 90
Lyon, Phyllis, 22, 83, 105
Lyon-Martin Lesbian/Gay
    Parenting Services
    (LGPS), 105
Lyon-Martin Women's Health
    Services, 105

MacKellen, Ian, 58
Martin, Del, 22, 83, 105
Mattachine Society, 83
Monette, Paul, 91

National Center for Lesbian
    Rights, 22, 97
National Gay and Lesbian
    Task Force, 86. *See
    also* National Gay Task
    Force
National Gay Task Force, 84,

86. *See also* National
    Gay and Lesbian Task
    Force
National Marches on Wash-
    ington for Lesbian and
    Gay Rights, 70, 86–87,
    101
Navratilova, Martina, 58
Nuclear-family model, 18, 20

Overlooked Opinions, 22

Pacific Reproductive Ser-
    vices, 105
Parent Groups, 103–105
Partners, 23
Patterson, Charlotte, 22,
    25–26, 29
Phelps, Fred, 92
Philadelphia, 91
Price, Deb, 91

"Religious Right," 92
Rich, Adrienne, 91

Second-parent adoption, 35,
    53
Sexual orientation, 21, 22,
    25, 27, 29, 30, 35, 36,
    37, 40, 56, 57, 66, 69,
    70, 71, 83, 86, 96
Single parent families, 18,
    19, 20, 24, 26, 29, 53,
    55, 55, 70, 74, 76, 94
Sodomy laws, 84, 87

ABOUT THE AUTHOR

Jill S. Pollack is a writer and editor whose work has appeared in newspapers, magazines, trade periodicals, and political journals. A graduate of The George Washington University, Ms. Pollack has worked on political campaigns and with political action committees, and is currently writing a book about women in politics. She is also the author of *Shirley Chisholm*, a Franklin Watts First Book. Ms. Pollack is a grant writer for the gay and lesbian social service agency Horizons in Chicago.